T0103307

WISE WORDS *from* KING CHARLES III

Also by Karen Dolby

The Wicked Wit of Queen Elizabeth II
The Wicked Wit of Prince Philip
The Wicked Wit of Princess Margaret
The Wicked Wit of The Royal Family

WISE WORDS *from* KING CHARLES III

Compiled by Karen Dolby

Michael O'Mara Books Limited

First published in Great Britain in 2024 by
Michael O'Mara Books Limited
9 Lion Yard
Tremadoc Road
London SW4 7NQ

A CIP catalogue record for this book is available from the British Library.

This product is made of material from well-managed, FSC®-certified forests and other controlled sources. The manufacturing processes conform to the environmental regulations of the country of origin.

ISBN: 978-1-78929-623-5 in hardback print format
ISBN: 978-1-78929-624-2 in ebook format

1 2 3 4 5 6 7 8 9 10

Cover design by Claire Cater, using a photograph from Vibrant Pictures / Alamy Stock Photo
Designed and typeset by Claire Cater
Printed and bound by CPI Group (UK) Ltd, Croydon, CR0 4YY

www.mombooks.com

MIX
Paper | Supporting
responsible forestry
FSC
www.fsc.org
FSC® C171272

Contents

Introduction

Charles Philip Arthur George, Prince of Wales and heir apparent for more than seventy years, became King of the United Kingdom and Commonwealth on 8 September 2022. On 6 May the following year the world watched as he was crowned at Westminster Abbey in a historic ceremony full of ritual and pageantry. *Wise Words From King Charles III* looks at the personality behind the pomp.

There was no set role for the heir to the British throne and, as Prince of Wales, it was very much left to Charles to carve out his own niche. He realized early on that he was in a unique position and that, unlike his mother Queen Elizabeth II, he had the freedom to speak out on the issues that concerned him. As he himself admitted, 'I'm a dangerous person because I mind about things.'

Charles has written books, made speeches and spoken out in interviews and documentaries. While the Queen famously kept a dignified silence on her private opinions, it seems that we know a great deal about our new sovereign's ideas. Though more guarded than his notoriously outspoken father, Charles has not been averse to sparking controversy with his views on the subjects close to his heart. During his years as king-in-waiting, there was plenty of time for his interests and personality to develop. Passionate about the environment and natural world, he was a conservationist, speaking out about climate change before it became the norm to do so. He felt he had no choice: 'I don't want my grandchildren or yours to come along and say to me, "Why the hell didn't you do something; you knew what the problem was."'

A skilled horticulturalist, he embraced his eccentric image and relished his reputation for talking to plants: 'I happily talk to plants and trees and listen to them. I think it's absolutely crucial.'

He is also a keen sportsman and music lover, and is interested in the arts and architecture. His views on modern buildings have prompted some of his most colourful comments. He famously called the proposed extension to the National Gallery in Trafalgar Square 'a monstrous carbuncle …'

After decades of being mocked for his views, his ideas on sustainable living, organic farming and environmentalism are all largely accepted as mainstream. In fact, he now seems something of a visionary.

Taking on a major new role at an age when most people would be retiring, King Charles brings a lifetime's wisdom and experience to the job. He has emphasized that his reign represents continuity and stability. The formal coronation service and his solemn pledge to 'uphold the constitutional principles at the heart of our nation' showed this is a monarch who still favours tradition.

He has ruled out being an 'activist king'. Instead, he has found ways to use soft power to great effect to continue influencing the issues that he has long cared passionately about, especially around how we treat our planet. This was apparent from his first two state visits as sovereign, to Germany and France, and the historic speeches he made to the parliaments of both countries. It is also reflected in his social initiatives, his wish for his coronation to encourage volunteering through the Big Help Out and the launch of the Coronation Food Project which aims to tackle the problems of food waste and poverty.

His stalwart sense of duty was never more in evidence than at the start of 2024 when the Royal Family faced a number of serious health issues. Announcements that the Princess of Wales was undergoing abdominal surgery at the same time that King Charles was to be treated for a benign enlarged prostate were closely followed by news of the King's cancer diagnosis for an unspecified form of the disease. In his first official statement after beginning treatment, King Charles thanked everyone for the many messages of support he had received and said, 'As all who have been affected by cancer will know, such kind thoughts are the greatest comfort and encouragement. It is equally heartening to hear how sharing my own diagnosis has helped promote public understanding and shine a light on the work of all those organizations which support cancer patients and their families across the UK and wider world. My lifelong admiration for their tireless care and dedication is all the greater as a result of my own personal experience.'

This book does not set out to tell the King's life story; there are scores of excellent biographies that do just that. Nor does it follow the intricacies of his relationships. Instead, it focuses on the causes, interests and ideas that have inspired the new King throughout his life, told through his own wise – and occasionally not so wise – words.

Timeline
of King Charles III's Life

1948   Prince Charles Philip Arthur George is born at 21:14 on 14 November to Princess Elizabeth (the future Queen Elizabeth II) and Prince Philip of Greece. He is christened on 15 December in the Music Room at Buckingham Palace. At the time, home is Windlesham Moor, near Windsor Castle.

1949   The young family move to Clarence House in London on 4 July, but when Philip becomes First Lieutenant of the destroyer HMS *Chequers*, they move to Malta, to the Villa Guardamangia, where they live for several months.

1950   Charles' younger sister Princess Anne, the Princess Royal, is born on 15 August at Clarence House.

1952   Elizabeth is proclaimed Queen on 6 February on the death of her father King George VI.

1953   Queen Elizabeth II's coronation takes place on 2 June at Westminster Abbey. A young Prince Charles watches with his grandmother the Queen Mother. In November, Charles and Anne stay behind in Britain while their parents begin a six-month tour of the Commonwealth. When Charles turns five, Catherine Peebles is appointed as his governess.

1956   Charles begins school at Hill House, London on 7 November.

1957   In September at the start of the new school year, Charles becomes a boarder at Cheam School in Berkshire.

1958   Queen Elizabeth II announces in July that Charles is to be Prince of Wales. He is the twenty-first person to be given the title.

1960   Prince Andrew is born on 19 February.

1962   At the start of the summer term in April, Charles begins school at Gordonstoun in Moray, North-East Scotland.

1964   Prince Edward is born on 10 March.

1965   Charles attends his first public engagement, a student garden party at the Palace of Holyroodhouse.

1966   Charles spends two terms at Timbertop School in Australia, the wilderness outpost of Geelong Church of England Grammar School near Melbourne.

1967   In September, Charles goes to Trinity College Cambridge, initially studying Anthropology and Archaeology before changing to History and the British Constitution.

1969   His Investiture as Prince of Wales takes place at Caernafon Castle on 1 July. In the run-up to the ceremony, Charles spends a term at Aberystwyth University.

1970   Charles makes his first important public speech addressing the Countryside in 1970 Committee for Wales, talking about the environment, conservation and the dangers of pollution. He graduates from Cambridge with a 2:2 and takes up his seat in the House of Lords.

1971   Charles joins the RAF in March and then the Royal Navy in September. He is presented with his RAF wings in August. Midway through the year, he meets Camilla Shand at the home of a mutual friend, Lucia Santa Cruz.

1974   On 13 June, Charles delivers his maiden speech in the House of Lords.

1976   In February, Charles takes command of HMS *Bronington* for his final ten months of service with the RN. The Prince's Trust charity is founded.

1977   Visiting Althorp with Lady Sarah Spencer, Charles meets Diana for the first time.

1980   In July, Charles meets Lady Diana Spencer again. He buys Highgrove House in Gloucestershire.

1981   24 February, Charles and Diana's engagement is announced.

On 29 July, their wedding takes place at St Paul's Cathedral. Millions watch worldwide.

1982 Prince William is born on 21 June. He becomes second in line to the throne after his father.

1984 Prince Harry is born on 15 September.

1986 Charles begins converting the gardens and farm estate at Highgrove to organic principles.

1992 The Queen's *annus horribilis*. Scandals rock the royal family, including the publication of Andrew Morton's biography of Diana revealing her personal struggles and marital problems. In December, Prime Minister John Major announces that the Prince and Princess of Wales are to legally separate.

1994 Charles is interviewed by Jonathan Dimbleby and speaks about his relationship with Camilla Parker Bowles in a programme broadcast on ITV.

1995 Charles becomes the first member of the royal family to visit the Republic of Ireland in an official capacity. *Panorama's* interview with Princess Diana about her marriage airs in November.

1996 Charles and Diana divorce on 28 August.

1997 Diana is killed in a car crash in Paris on 31 August. A huge outpouring of public grief follows and her funeral on 6 September is watched by over 32 million people in the UK.

2002   On 9 February Princess Margaret dies and the Queen Mother just six weeks later, on 30 March. Queen Elizabeth II's Golden Jubilee celebrations start in April.

2005   Charles and Camilla are married on 9 April in a civil ceremony at Windsor Guildhall followed by a religious blessing at St George's Chapel, Windsor Castle.

2011   On 29 April, Prince William and Catherine Middleton are married at Westminster Abbey.

2013   Prince William and Catherine's first child, Prince George, is born on 22 July. He is Charles's first grandchild and becomes third in line to the throne, after his father and grandfather.

2015   Their second child, Princess Charlotte, is born on 2 May.

2017   Prince Philip announces that he is stepping down from public duty, making his final solo engagement at a Royal Marines parade in August.

2018   On 23 April, Prince William and Catherine's youngest child, Prince Louis, is born. On 19 May the wedding of Prince Harry and Meghan Markle is held at St George's Chapel, Windsor Castle.

2019   Archie Harrison, Prince Harry and Meghan's first child is born on 6 May.

2020   In January, Buckingham Palace announces that Prince Harry is to step back from Royal duties, including his military appointments, and in March that the Duke and Duchess of Sussex will no longer undertake official Royal engagements. The couple move to the US and buy a house in Montecito, California in June.

2021   Prince Philip dies on 9 April. His funeral takes place at St George's Chapel, Windsor Castle. Prince Harry and Meghan's second child, Lilibet, is born on 4 June.

2022   In May, Charles delivers the Queen's Speech at the State Opening of Parliament, acting on her behalf as a counsellor of state. On 8 September, Charles becomes King on the death of his mother. He is formally proclaimed monarch on 11 September at the Accession Council ceremony. He makes his first speech to the country at 6pm on 9 September. Queen Elizabeth's state funeral and procession take place on 19 September with a ceremony at Westminster Abbey.

2023   King Charles and Queen Camilla are crowned at Westminster Abbey on 6 May. In March, the couple make the first state visit of Charles' reign to Germany, where he becomes the first British monarch to address the Bundestag. He repeats this first during his state visit to France in September when he addresses the Senate.

'It has just been announced from Buckingham Palace that Her Royal Highness Princess Elizabeth, Duchess of Edinburgh, has safely delivered a prince at 9:14 p.m. and that Her Royal Highness and her son are both doing well. Listeners will wish us to offer their loyal congratulations to Princess Elizabeth and to the royal family on this happy occasion.'

FRANKLIN ENGELMANN, BBC RADIO ANNOUNCER, 14 NOVEMBER 1948.

The Young Prince

From the first, Prince Charles Philip Arthur George was in the public eye, the target of intense interest and speculation, every stage of his life documented and photographed. Major Thomas Harvey, private secretary to Charles's grandmother Queen Elizabeth the Queen Mother commented, 'Poor little chap, two-and-a-half hours after being born, he was being looked at by outsiders.'

Four thousand congratulatory telegrams arrived on the night of Charles's birth while a huge crowd gathered outside Buckingham Palace to celebrate and party into the night.

His father reckoned he looked just like 'a plum pudding', while his mother noticed his hands, 'He has large hands but fine with long fingers – quite unlike mine and certainly unlike his father's. It will be interesting to see what they will become.'

Schooldays
and Education

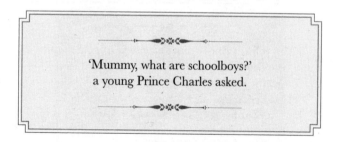

'Mummy, what are schoolboys?'
a young Prince Charles asked.

His first lessons took place at home under the supervision of his Scottish governess, Catherine Peebles. She quickly recognized his sensitive nature and insecurities, how he shrank from raised voices. During his annual visit to Balmoral, Prime Minister Winston Churchill also had the opportunity to watch the four-year-old heir to the throne, commenting, 'He's young to think so much.'

Prince Philip explained, 'The Queen and I want Charles to go to school with other boys of his generation and learn to live with other children, and to absorb the discipline imposed by education with others.'

Prince Philip's experience of school had always been a positive one. For him school represented stability. It was a safe constant in what had been a chaotic childhood from the very start, when he was hurriedly smuggled out of Greece in an orange box as a young baby. Separated from his parents, he'd learned to 'just get on with it', believing that challenges had made him resourceful. However, his eldest son was a very different character with a different experience of family.

Charles's nanny Mabel Anderson observed, 'He felt family separation very deeply. He dreaded going away to school.' He was the first heir to the throne to be educated outside of the palace.

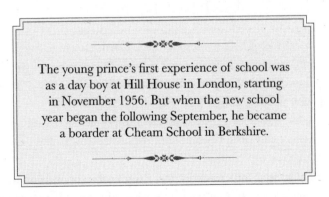

The young prince's first experience of school was as a day boy at Hill House in London, starting in November 1956. But when the new school year began the following September, he became a boarder at Cheam School in Berkshire.

Writing his first letter home, he had no idea how to address it. 'I know my mother is Queen, but how do I put that on the envelope?' It may have been his parents' wish that Charles be treated just like any other pupil, but his position and title obviously marked him out, and he was painfully aware of the differences. 'I wish they prayed for the other boys too,' he said of the morning prayers for the royal family, including himself.

At the Commonwealth Games held in Cardiff in July 1958, the Queen announced that she was giving her eldest son the title Prince of Wales.

'I remember being acutely embarrassed when it was announced,' Charles said, looking back. He had listened to the broadcast on the radio at Cheam School. 'I heard this marvellous great cheer coming from the stadium in Cardiff, and I think for a little boy of nine it was rather bewildering. All the others turned and looked at me in amazement.'

Colditz in Kilts

If Charles found his prep school hard, Gordonstoun in north-east Scotland was in a whole different league. This was his father's old school and Philip had loved his time there. In May 1962, Philip flew with Charles to Scotland and then drove him the rest of the way to his new boarding school. Gordonstoun had a reputation for toughness and Prince Charles once described it as 'Colditz in kilts' and 'A prison of privilege'.

The Queen Mother worried that the school was not ideally suited to her sensitive grandson: 'He is a very gentle boy, with a very kind heart, which I think is the essence of everything.'

Prince Philip thought otherwise: 'Children may be indulged at home, but school is expected to be a Spartan and disciplined experience in the process of developing into self-controlled, considerate and independent adults.'

After two years there Charles wrote a letter home that pulled no punches on the everyday horrors of his life at Gordonstoun, 'It's such hell here especially at night. I don't get any sleep practically at all nowadays … The people in my dormitory are foul. Goodness they are horrid, I don't know how anyone could be so foul. They throw slippers all night long or hit me with pillows or rush across the room and hit me as hard as they can, then beetle back again as fast as they can, waking up everyone else in the dormitory at the same time. I still wish I could come home. It's such a hole this place!'

Charles later echoed his nanny, Mabel Anderson's, view, 'I did not enjoy school as much as I might have, but this was because I am happier at home than anywhere else.'

He also said looking back at his years at Gordonstoun, 'I had this schoolboy dream that I was going to escape and hide in the forest, in a place where no one could find me, so that I wouldn't have to go back to school. I hated that institution, just as I hated leaving home. When you lead a perfectly agreeable existence you don't want to go back to cold showers at seven in the morning and a quick run before breakfast.'

On a more positive note, in an echo of his father's views on the purpose of schooling, he added, 'Gordonstoun developed my will-power and self-control, helped me to discipline myself, and I think that discipline, not in the sense of making you bath in cold water, but in the Latin sense – giving shape and form and tidiness to your life is the most important thing your education can do.'

Pommy Prince

Gordonstoun remained challenging for the young prince, but the two terms he spent at Timbertop in Australia he found truly liberating. This school was the wilderness campus of Geelong Church of England Grammar School in Melbourne. While there, for the first time seventeen-year-old Charles felt judged 'on how people see you, and feel about you,' rather than on his title. 'There are no assumptions. You have to fend for yourself.'

He thrived on the informality and the physical challenges set for the pupils, writing enthusiastically about his experiences there: 'The first week I was here, I was made to go out and chop logs on a hillside in boiling hot weather. I could hardly see my hands for blisters.'

On Australian insects, he commented, 'You virtually have to inspect every inch of the ground you hope to put your tent on in case there are any ants or other ghastly creatures. There is one species of ant called Bull Ants which are three-quarters of an inch long, and they bite like mad.'

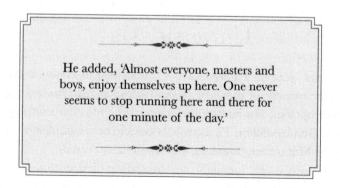

He added, 'Almost everyone, masters and boys, enjoy themselves up here. One never seems to stop running here and there for one minute of the day.'

While at the school, he also undertook a number of official engagements in front of big crowds for the first time on his own. 'I took the plunge and went over and talked to people. That suddenly unlocked a completely different feeling and I was then able to communicate and talk to people so much more.'

'I absolutely adored it,' Charles said of his months in Australia. 'Quite frankly, it was by far the best part of my education. While I was there, I had the pommy bits bashed off me. Like chips off an old block.'

David Checketts, Prince Philip's equerry who was assigned to accompany the young prince during his time away, put it simply, 'I went out there with a boy and returned with a man.'

It was also during his schooldays that Charles developed many of the ideas and interests that would stay with him for life – among them a taste for acting and comedy, a passion for music and playing the cello, and an interest in Plato, particularly his vision of a philosopher king.

University Days

Charles went to Trinity College Cambridge in October 1967. To the surprise of many, he began by studying Archaeology and Anthropology. His interest had been sparked by a visit to Papua New Guinea while at Timbertop school and by archaeological digs in the Morayshire caves near Gordonstoun.

He explained, 'I thought, here's a chance I'll never have again: to do something pre-history, get to know about the earlier societies and the most primitive kinds of men.' He also had the idea that, 'If more people can be assisted to appreciate and understand their own social behaviour, the better and more healthy our society will be.'

He switched to History, studying the British Constitution for the second part of his degree, 'Because I'm probably going to be King.'

Of his university days Charles said it had been, 'Marvellous to have three years when you are not bound by anything, and not married, and haven't got any particular job.'

During his time at Cambridge, the traditionally strict curfew rules governing the hour at which the college gates were closed each night were relaxed. The prince rather regretted this, commenting, 'It was a great challenge to climb over the wall. Half the fun of university life is breaking the rules.'

Prince of Wales

Charles also spent a term at the University College of Wales at Aberystwyth, studying Welsh history and language in preparation for his investiture as Prince of Wales at Caernarfon Castle on 1 July 1969.

In spite of a warm welcome by the majority of Welsh people, his arrival at the Welsh university was met with some opposition. He later said of the experience, 'Most days there seemed to be a demonstration going on against me, usually by splendid middle-aged ladies who got out of a bus … I did my utmost to learn as much Welsh as I could which in a term is quite difficult and I am not as brilliant a linguist as I would like to be. But my being there for that period made an enormous difference to my understanding of the way Wales works and what I did pick up particularly was an immense sense of real community. It is a wonderful mosaic that I think makes the principality so special.'

While there, he came to appreciate the Welsh countryside and learned enough of the language to deliver a seven-minute speech in Welsh at a youth festival. The audience of six thousand gave the young prince a standing ovation.

Afterwards, writing to a friend, Charles again commented on the insight he felt he'd gained: 'If I have learned anything during the last eight weeks, it's been about Wales. They feel so strongly about Wales as a nation, and it means something to them, and they are depressed by what might happen to it if they don't try and preserve the language and the culture, which is unique and special to Wales, and if something is unique and special, I see it as well worth preserving.'

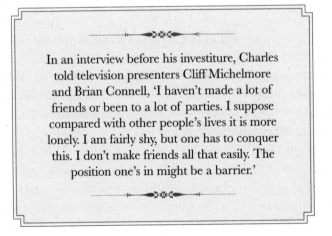

In an interview before his investiture, Charles told television presenters Cliff Michelmore and Brian Connell, 'I haven't made a lot of friends or been to a lot of parties. I suppose compared with other people's lives it is more lonely. I am fairly shy, but one has to conquer this. I don't make friends all that easily. The position one's in might be a barrier.'

Serving Queen and Country

After graduating, Charles joined the RAF as a flight lieutenant in March 1971 and then a few months later, in September, joined the Royal Navy as acting sub-lieutenant.

While still at university he had said, 'Time in the services is a very good idea. It gives one a useful experience, a sense of discipline and responsibility. A sense of responsibility is the most important thing.'

He had thought carefully about his decision, 'It is pointless and ill-informed to say that I am entering a profession trained in killing. The Services in the first place are there for fast, efficient and well-trained action in defence. Surely the Services must attract a large number of duty-conscious people? Otherwise who else would subject themselves to being square-bashed, shouted at by petty officers and made to do ghastly things in Force Ten gales? I am entering the RAF and then the Navy because I believe I can contribute something to this country by so doing. To me it is a worthwhile occupation, and one which I am convinced will stand me in good stead for the rest of my life.'

Charles had taken flying lessons at university with Squadron Leader Philip Pinney and he flew himself to RAF Cranwell in Lincolnshire to begin his four-month attachment there. As always, royal protocol and security needs complicated matters, and he was not allowed to take part in certain operations that other young officers undertook as part of their training.

He wrote, 'How strange it seems to be a serving officer all of a sudden. I am now just beginning to get used to the fact that I have a uniform on and I ought to be calling senior officers "Sir". The latter I find most difficult because I haven't called anyone "Sir" for a long time … They seem more nervous of me than I do of them – but I dare say the element of fear and subservience will soon return to me via the agency of a well-placed boot!'

Nevertheless, he enjoyed his time at Cranwell and later also relished the chance to widen his experience on board ship with the Royal Navy, 'It's given me a marvellous opportunity to get as close to the "Ordinary" British chap as possible.' Though he did once jokingly threaten some of those 'ordinary chaps' who were trying to de-bag him with an archaic royal punishment, 'I can send you to the Tower you know. It's quite within my power.'

In Command

In February 1976, Charles took command of HMS *Bronington*, a coastal minesweeper, for his final ten months of service with the Royal Navy. He wrote in his diary, 'The whole prospect weighed heavily upon me as I drove across the Forth Bridge. There seemed so many things to worry about, particularly as I am not the sort of person who is endowed with supreme self-confidence. Starting off somewhere new is always an effort, not to mention meeting new people and wondering what the officers were going to be like.'

A fortnight later he sounded far more confident in a letter to his great-uncle Lord Louis Mountbatten: 'It really does seem quite extraordinary to be sitting here as Captain of this ship! You really were absolutely right (as usual) – you do feel frightfully grand and not a little confused. Fortunately a considerable proportion of the confusion has worn off since last week and I am now enjoying the whole experience of "being in command".'

HMS *Bronington*'s routine role was to follow a plotted course, using sonar to detect any underwater mines. Charles noted in his diary, 'A large part of our operations at the moment is excruciatingly dull. I spent twelve hours non-stop on the bridge the other night while we were mine-hunting and felt like dying quietly then and there.'

After an exercise in the Baltic, Charles found himself wishing he could die for different reasons. The ship hit storm-force winds and a raging gale. 'Never in my life have I felt so ill or been so appallingly sick as I was that day and night,' he commented. 'I found myself quite happy at the prospect of the ship quietly turning over and sinking – I was well beyond the point of caring ...'

But the responsibility of the job also weighed heavily on the prince: 'I've already aged ten years since I took over the ship and keep waking up at night (at sea and on shore) convinced we are dragging the anchor or something ghastly has gone wrong.'

Looking back at this period in command Charles said, 'I spent most of the time petrified that I was going to run aground or we'd have a collision or some major horror like that because I knew that all these people from the media were just waiting like sharks for the kill.'

Although he took time out for royal duties, he served until the end of 1976, by which time he had been promoted to wing commander in the RAF and commander in the Navy. He had been a popular and competent commanding officer, and his final

Naval report paid tribute to his 'deep understanding for his sailors and their families and their problems and as a result the morale of his ship has been of an extremely high order.'

'As the Queen herself did with such unswerving devotion, I, too, now solemnly pledge myself, throughout the remaining time God grants me, to uphold the constitutional principles at the heart of our nation.'

KING CHARLES III ADDRESSING THE NATION ON HIS
ACCESSION TO THE THRONE IN SEPTEMBER 2022.

Being Royal

King Charles was not only the longest serving, and oldest, Prince of Wales in British history, holding the title for sixty-four years and forty-four days, he is also the oldest person to succeed to the British throne. He was seventy-three. The record was previously held by King William IV who became monarch in 1830 at the age of sixty-four years.

Charles's position as heir to the throne meant that from an early age he was under no illusions about the reality of what it meant to be royal. 'I didn't suddenly wake up in my pram one day and say "Yippee!" It just dawns on you slowly that people are interested … and slowly you get the idea that you have a certain duty and responsibility. It's better that way, rather than someone suddenly telling you "You must do this" and "You must do that", because of who you are. It's one of those things you grow up in,' he explained in a BBC radio interview in 1969.

Queen Who?

When a palace courtier told Charles, who was then not quite four years old that he was on his way to see the Queen, the young prince innocently asked, 'Who's she?'

Looking back, he reflected, 'I learned the way a monkey learns, by watching its parents.' But there is no particular training for the heir to the throne. 'You pick it up as you go along. You watch and learn.'

Just before his twenty-first birthday, Charles was asked when he first realized that he was heir to the throne. He replied, 'I think it's something that dawns on you with the most ghastly inexorable sense … and slowly you get the idea that you have a certain duty and responsibility.'

Acutely aware of his unique position and everyone's expectations, Charles commented, 'All the time I felt I must justify my existence.' When questioned about being royal, Prince Charles reckoned, 'I am, at best, nothing more than a travelling ambassador for Britain.'

Prince in Waiting

After a royal tour to Canada and the USA in 1970, Charles reflected on a conversation he had with President Richard Nixon about his role as heir apparent: 'To be just a presence would be fatal … I know lots of Americans think one's main job is to go around saying meaningless niceties, but a presence alone can be swept away so easily.'

'I have been brought up to have an active role,' he once told journalists. 'I am determined not to be confined to cutting ribbons.'

Prince Charles once jokingly described the monarchy as, 'The oldest profession in the world.' He also said, 'Were it not for my ability to see the funny side of my life, I would have been committed to an institution long ago.'

He was perhaps thinking of this when he remarked, 'What I have to do for England!'

When asked about his position as prince in waiting, Charles reflected, 'I am heir to the throne. Full stop. That is all. I could do absolutely nothing if I wanted to. I could go and play polo all over the world.'

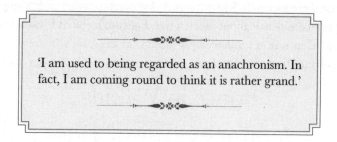

'I am used to being regarded as an anachronism. In fact, I am coming round to think it is rather grand.'

It may be a dubious distinction to be the oldest as well as the longest-serving heir to the throne in British history, but this has given Charles a long time to consider his role. He has spoken on the subject many times, once saying, 'There is no set-out role for me. It depends entirely what I make of it … I'm really rather an awkward problem.'

While still a student at Cambridge University he had spoken quite openly on the subject: 'My great problem in life is that I do not really know what my role in life is. At the moment I do not have one. But somehow I must find one.'

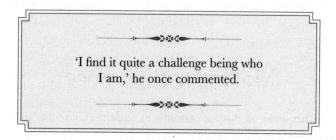

'I find it quite a challenge being who I am,' he once commented.

Rather than dictating his views, he thought, 'I can only go muddling along pursuing the sort of things I think are right and true, and hope there's a result. I'm not somebody overburdened with a sense of self-confidence about such things. I always feel that I should be somewhat reticent, otherwise you end up thinking you are more important than you are. I just go on trying to encourage, to help.'

A Strong Sense of Duty

Never complacent, he was hardly one to sit back and enjoy the privileges of royalty. He saw it as his duty to make a positive contribution.

Interviewed by *Time* magazine in 2013, Charles revealed, 'I've had this extraordinary feeling, for years and years, ever since I can remember really, of wanting to heal and make things better. I feel more than anything else it's my duty to worry about everybody and their lives in this country, to try to find a way of improving things if I possibly can.'

At the same time when asked about the idea of bypassing him as rightful heir to the throne in favour of Prince William, Charles said, 'If you chuck away too many things, you end up discovering there was value in them.'

Making a Difference

It was his sense of duty and desire to make a difference that lay behind his decision towards the end of 1976, when he was not quite thirty, to leave the Navy. While considering the move, he wrote, 'Perhaps I'm wrong or have an over-inflated sense of my own importance, but I feel I could be more useful at home than miles away.'

Various jobs were put forward as possibilities for the young prince, including governor-general of Australia and British ambassador to France. Neither role was really appropriate for the heir to the throne. There was no shortage of public engagements but it was clear there was no defined job. If Charles wanted to be useful and make a difference, he would need to carve out his own path.

He was already active in many areas. He was involved in the running of the Duchy of Cornwall, the Prince of Wales Environment Committee for Wales and the United World Colleges (an organization that sought to establish a network of international schools for potential leaders of diverse nationalities). He was also chancellor of the University of Wales, colonel-in-chief of five British regiments, and had a role in a growing number of patronages. To this list he soon added The Prince's Trust youth charity (now The King's Trust).

Nevertheless, Charles sometimes found himself frustrated by the limitations imposed on him. A couple of years after leaving the Navy he wrote, 'I want to consider ways in which I can escape from the ceaseless round of official engagements and meet people in less artificial circumstances. In other words, I want to look at the possibility of spending, say, 1. Three days in one factory to find out what happens; 2. Three days, perhaps, in a trawler (instead of one rapid visit); 3. Three or four days on a farm. I would also like to consider 4. More visits to immigrant areas in order to help these people to feel that they are not ignored or neglected and that we are concerned about them as individuals.'

Writing home to friends during a tour of New Zealand in 1981, his general frustration on the restrictions and repetitive nature of many of his royal duties is very obvious, 'I am beginning to get fed up with the amount of nonsensical rubbish I take all day and every day. If one more NZ child asks me what it's like to be a prince, I shall go demented.'

Ich Dien

Musing on the traditional motto of the Prince of Wales – '*Ich Dien*', meaning 'I serve' – Prince Charles reflected, '"I serve" is a marvellous motto to have. That is the basis of one's job. If you have a sense of duty, and I like to think I have, then service is something that you give to people, particularly if they want you – but sometimes if they don't.' He has also said, 'I can't affect things on a large scale. The only way I can see myself achieving anything is by example.'

Speaking in 1981, he explained his position as he saw it, 'A Prince of Wales has to do what he can by influence. Not power. There isn't any power, but there can be influence. The influence you have is in direct ratio to the respect people have for you.'

He pointed out, 'I could have sat doing very little indeed and

I would have been got at just as much by people saying, "What a useless idiot he is." So I would rather be criticized for doing things rather than not doing them.'

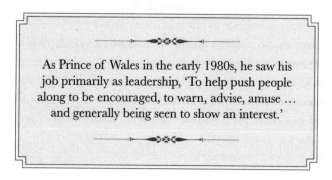

As Prince of Wales in the early 1980s, he saw his job primarily as leadership, 'To help push people along to be encouraged, to warn, advise, amuse … and generally being seen to show an interest.'

In an interview with the American television news programme *60 Minutes* in 2005, he explained, 'I find myself born into this particular position. I'm determined to make the most of it and to do whatever I can to help. And I hope I leave things behind a little better than I found them.'

He told *Time* magazine, 'I feel more than anything else it's my duty to worry about everybody and their lives in this country, to try to find a way of improving things if I possibly can.'

Less positively, the prince spoke about the predictability that is always a part of his role: 'You can't understand what it's like to have your whole life mapped out for you a year in advance. It's so awful to be programmed. I know what I'll be doing next week, next month, even next year. At times I get so fed up with the whole idea.'

The Monarchy

In an interview with Jonathan Dimbleby in 1994, broadcast on ITV, Charles was candid when asked about the future of the monarchy: 'Something as curious as the monarchy won't survive unless you take account of people's attitudes. After all, if people don't want it, they won't have it.'

In the same interview, thinking ahead to what it might be like to be king, he mused, 'Sometimes you daydream about the sort of things you might do … I think you could invest the position with something of your own personality and interest but obviously within the bounds of constitutional propriety.'

In November 2008, just before his sixtieth birthday, the BBC aired the documentary portrait *A Passionate Prince*. In the programme, Charles was asked if he enjoyed his role. He appeared slightly uncertain: 'Well, I don't know. Bits of it. It is something that I felt I must do – to help as many other people as I possibly can in this country.'

Asked about the ceremonial trappings of monarchy, Prince Charles said, 'I would change nothing. Besides ceremony being a major and important aspect of monarchy, something that has grown and developed over a thousand years in Britain, I happen to enjoy it enormously.' However, he has also admitted that he would like to modernize 'the old remote image of royalty', and has frequently referred to his preference for a 'slimmed down' monarchy.

From Prince to King

During the making of the BBC documentary *Prince, Son and Heir: Charles at 70*, filmmaker John Bridcut asked whether the Prince would continue with his public campaigns after he became King. Charles was direct in his reply: 'No … I'm not that stupid. I do realize that it is a separate exercise being sovereign. So of course, I understand entirely how that should operate.'

He went on, 'The idea somehow, that I'm going to go on in exactly the same way, if I succeed, is complete nonsense because the two – the two situations – are completely different.'

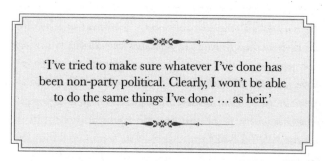

'I've tried to make sure whatever I've done has been non-party political. Clearly, I won't be able to do the same things I've done … as heir.'

When pushed about his reputation for occasionally meddling, Charles laughed before adding, 'I always wonder what meddling is. I mean, I always thought it was motivating but I've always been intrigued: if it's meddling to worry about the inner cities as I did forty years ago and what was happening or not happening there, the conditions in which people were living … If that's meddling, I'm very proud of it.'

Charles's address to the nation on 9 September 2022, the day after his mother's death, was a loving tribute to Britain's longest serving monarch:

'Alongside the personal grief that all my family are feeling we also share with so many of you in the United Kingdom, in all the countries where the Queen was Head of State, in the Commonwealth and across the world, a deep sense of gratitude for the more than seventy years in which my mother, as Queen, served the people of so many nations. In 1947, on her twenty-first birthday, she pledged in a broadcast from Cape Town to the Commonwealth to devote her life, whether it be short or long, to the service of her peoples. That was more than a promise: it was a profound personal commitment which defined her whole life. She made sacrifices for duty. Her dedication and devotion as sovereign never wavered, through times of change and progress, through times of joy and celebration, and times of sadness and loss. In her life of service, we saw that abiding love of tradition, together with that fearless embrace of progress, which make us great as nations. The affection, admiration and respect she inspired became the hallmark of her reign ... and she combined these qualities with warmth, humour, and an unerring ability always to see the best in people.'

He went on to express some of his own intentions as King:

'... Through all changes and challenges, our nation, and the wider family of realms – of whose talents, traditions and achievements I am so inexpressibly proud – have prospered and flourished. Our values remained, and must remain, constant.

The role and duties of monarchy also remain, as does the sovereign's particular relationship and responsibility toward the Church of

England – the church in which my own faith is so deeply rooted. In that faith, and the values it inspires, I have been brought up to cherish a sense of duty to others, and to hold in the greatest respect the precious traditions, freedoms and responsibilities of our unique history and our system of parliamentary government.

'As the Queen herself did with such unswerving devotion, I too now solemnly pledge myself, throughout the remaining time God grants me, to uphold the constitutional principles at the heart of our nation. And wherever you may live in the United Kingdom, or in the realms and territories across the world, and whatever may be your background or beliefs, I shall endeavour to serve you with loyalty, respect and love, as I have throughout my life.

'My life will of course change as I take up my new responsibilities. It will no longer be possible for me to give so much of my time and energies to the charities and issues for which I care so deeply. But I know this important work will go on in the trusted hands of others.'

King Charles III

Charles became King on 8 September 2022 but was formally proclaimed at the traditional Accession Council ceremony which was held at St James's Palace on 10 September. His ceremony was the first one to be filmed. As new sovereign he pledged, 'In carrying out the heavy task that has been laid upon me, to which I dedicate what remains to me of my life, I pray for the guidance and help of almighty God.'

On 16 September, addressing religious leaders at Buckingham Palace Charles spoke about his 'duty to protect the diversity of our country, including by protecting the space for Faith itself and its practice through the religions, cultures, traditions and beliefs to which our hearts and minds direct us.' He continued, 'My Christian beliefs have love at their very heart. By my most profound convictions, therefore, as well as by my position as sovereign, I hold myself bound to respect those who follow other spiritual paths, as well as those who seek to live their lives according to secular ideals.'

'I work bloody hard right now and will continue to.'

CHARLES AS PRINCE OF WALES, SPEAKING IN 1981.

Life's Work

Perhaps it was the work ethic instilled in him from an early age by his parents, or the strict regime he had to follow at Gordonstoun, but Charles has never been one to sit back and watch from the sidelines. He was determined to carve out a useful role for himself and to champion causes that he believed were important. As Prince of Wales, he was not afraid to speak out even if his views were unpopular. Interviewed in 2010, he defended his stance over the years, suggesting that if his parents and officials hadn't wanted him to think independently, they should not have 'sent me to a school which was precepted on taking the initiative. Or to a university where you inevitably look into a lot of these issues.'

Conservation and the Environment

Charles has been an outspoken campaigner for the environment for more than fifty years. It is significant that his first important public speech, while still a university student, was on the subject. And he didn't pull any punches.

He was addressing the 'Countryside in 1970' conference held by the Steering Committee for Wales in Cardiff and was appalled by 'the horrifying effects of pollution in all its cancerous forms'. He went on to explain, 'There is the growing menace of oil pollution at sea, which almost destroys beaches and certainly destroys tens of thousands of seabirds. There is chemical pollution discharged into rivers from factories and chemical plants, which clogs up the rivers with toxic substances and adds to the filth in the seas. There is air pollution from smoke and fumes discharged by factories and from gases pumped out by endless cars and aeroplanes.'

He was also one of the first to draw attention to the problem of plastic waste: 'When you think there are 55 million of us on this island using non-returnable bottles and indestructible plastic containers, it is not difficult to imagine the mountains of refuse that we shall have to deal with.'

Ahead of His Time

Charles called for a more joined-up approach to 'the total environment', something that has marked his outlook ever since:

'Conservation or problems about pollution should not be held up as separate concepts from housing or other social schemes. "Conservation" means being aware of the total environment that we live in … The word ecology implies the relationship of an organism to its environment and we are just as much an organism as any other animal that is often unfortunate enough to share this earth with us.'

His views may seem mainstream now, but they were considered radical in February 1970. The term 'global warming' wasn't part of the international vocabulary until scientist Wallace Broecker popularized it five years later. The young prince might have been following Prince Philip's lead as a committed conservationist, but he went much further than his famously outspoken father in expressing his thoughts.

Speaking in Canada in 1975, Charles again focussed on our relationship with the natural world. 'Our own particular civilization, if you can call it that, loses a great deal in an attempt to control nature. We must always remember that we are basically animals – and not to destroy all of nature, that is absolutely necessary.'

Initially mocked by the media and public, he was well aware of his eccentric reputation, 'In those early days I was described as old fashioned, out of touch and anti-science; a dreamer in a modern world.'

He was not deterred. He saw a responsible attitude towards care for the environment and climate change as too important, 'Like the sorcerer's apprentice causing havoc in his master's home when he couldn't control the spell which he had released, mankind runs a similar risk of laying waste his earthly home by thinking he's in control when he's clearly not.'

Inspiration

Charles has written that as a boy he was enthralled by the natural world. 'As far as I was concerned, every tree, every hedgerow, every wet place, every mountain and river had a special, almost sacred character of its own.'

The freedom he had from a young age to walk the hills and countryside of Scotland while staying on the Balmoral estate, or at Sandringham in Norfolk, left a lasting impression and set a blueprint for his interest in the environment.

On his mother's accession to the throne in 1952, the three-year-old Prince Charles automatically acquired many new titles including 'Lord of the Isles' about which he has commented, 'I'm an incurable romantic and it is a marvellously romantic title.'

Duty of Care

Years later, interviewed by the BBC for the documentary *Prince, Son and Heir: Charles at 70*, the then Prince of Wales explained that he saw speaking out as his 'constitutional duty'. He knew that as King he would not have the same opportunity for plain speaking.

'If you become the sovereign then you play the role in the way that it is expected. Clearly I won't be able to do the same things I've done as heir. So, of course, you operate within the constitutional parameters. But it's a different function.'

As Prince of Wales, Charles knew he had a unique platform to put forward his views on issues close to his heart, 'People come out of curiosity if nothing else.'

He was also well aware that every word he spoke or wrote would be scrutinized, 'I can tell you that writing speeches is a major sweat, worrying whether you're going to say the right thing, because everyone will jump on you.'

Charles has always been aware of a moral duty to protect the environment, 'I have rather subscribed to an outlook shared by many indigenous peoples that we must be thinking seven generations ahead really to have any chance to be sure that we leave a better world behind us.'

Writing in *Newsweek* magazine he warned, 'If we only maintain our rights now without acknowledging our responsibilities to those who come after us, then we would have failed to act morally.'

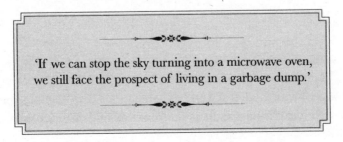

'If we can stop the sky turning into a microwave oven, we still face the prospect of living in a garbage dump.'

Environmentalism

Speaking on the subject in 2015 at the Paris climate change summit, Charles again stressed the importance of caring for our world: 'On an increasingly crowded planet, humanity faces many threats but none is greater than climate change. It magnifies every hazard and tension of our existence.'

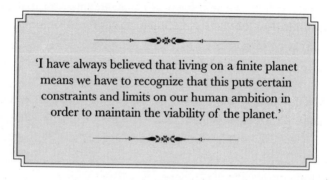

'I have always believed that living on a finite planet means we have to recognize that this puts certain constraints and limits on our human ambition in order to maintain the viability of the planet.'

Addressing business leaders in Dubai, he again warned of the very real danger of a climate disaster. 'We are facing what I believe is perhaps the greatest challenge ever faced by our economy and society. I have been finding the struggle somewhat exhausting and frustrating over the past twenty-five to thirty years to overcome the deniers and sceptics. If we are honest, we know all too clearly that we can't go on as we are.

At a Business in the Community Awards Dinner in 2007 he said, '… business is recognizing the role it can play in combatting climate change. Thank God, is all I can say, for there is a desperately urgent need for business to play that role. Your lobbying influence can be substantial, but together, united and in large enough numbers it could prove decisive in turning the tide.'

Charles was pragmatic about climate change: 'We need to be realistic,' he said in his Presidential Address in Indonesia in 2008. 'There is very little we can do now to stop the ice from disappearing from the North Pole in the summer. And we probably cannot prevent the melting of the permafrost and the resulting release of methane. In addition, I fear that we may be too late to help the oceans maintain their ability to absorb carbon dioxide.'

And he has suggested, 'We might be more inclined to think about the longer term if we were more aware of what is happening around us. Perhaps daily weather forecasts could include a few basic facts about the Earth's vital signs or details of where climate change is increasing the likelihood of damaging weather?'

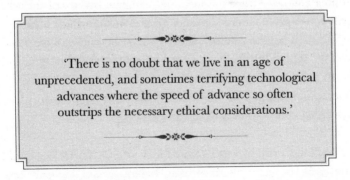

'There is no doubt that we live in an age of unprecedented, and sometimes terrifying technological advances where the speed of advance so often outstrips the necessary ethical considerations.'

Charles has wondered why humanity is not prepared for climate change to be worse than predicted: 'Scientists themselves readily admit that they do not fully understand the consequences of our many-faceted assault upon the interwoven fabric of atmosphere, water, land and life in all its biological diversity. But things could also turn out to be worse than the current scientific best guess. In military affairs, policy has long been based on the dictum that we should be prepared for the worst case. Why should it be so different when the security is that of the planet and our long-term future?'

Like Father, Like Sons

King Charles has been careful to pass on his sense of responsibility to his two sons. Ever practical, he taught both to switch off lights when they left a room. Prince William joked, 'I've got serious OCD on light switches.'

In the BBC documentary *Prince Charles at 70*, which aired in 2018, both William and Harry described how their father encouraged them to pick up litter. Prince Harry explained, 'He took us litter-picking when we were younger, on holiday … we thought this is perfectly normal, everyone must do it. We were there with our spikes, stabbing the rubbish into black plastic bags.'

Green King

Green long before it was fashionable, in 1986 Charles began the process of converting the gardens at Highgrove, his Gloucestershire home, and the nearby 900-acre Home Farm to organic principles. It has been a labour of love ever since.

When he first took over in the early 1980s, the gardens at Highgrove were badly neglected and overgrown. Charles set about redesigning them with advice from various experts, in particular Rosemary Verey, the renowned plantswoman and garden designer, and naturalist Miriam Rothschild. But it was his first garden teacher, Mollie Salisbury, who taught him the importance of speaking to his plants, a practice the King still follows.

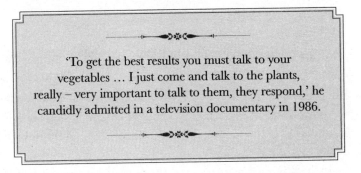

> 'To get the best results you must talk to your vegetables ... I just come and talk to the plants, really – very important to talk to them, they respond,' he candidly admitted in a television documentary in 1986.

Charles is convinced it makes a difference, and no amount of jokes at his expense have managed to convince him otherwise. He seems happy to raise a smile and play up to the slightly eccentric image: 'Only the other day I was inquiring of an entire bed of old-fashioned roses, forced to listen to my ramblings on the meaning of the universe as I sat cross-legged in the lotus position in front of them.'

When he opened the Millennium Seed Bank at Kew Gardens, the largest plant conservation programme in the world, Charles said, 'I want to make certain that I have some plants left to talk to.'

He claims to find weeding 'very therapeutic ... and it's marvellous if you can do enough to see the effect.' As a keen supporter of traditional crafts and skills, he has also learned how to lay hedges on the estate.

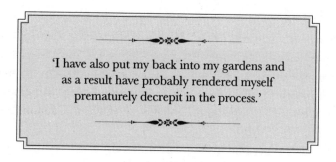

'I have also put my back into my gardens and as a result have probably rendered myself prematurely decrepit in the process.'

In the introduction to his book about the Highgrove Estate, he wrote in 1993, 'The garden at Highgrove really does spring from my heart and, strange as it may seem to some, creating it has been rather like a form of worship.'

Organic Principles –
Seer or Madman?

'I was told I was a complete idiot for even suggesting going organic,' Charles has commented.

In the early days it was not the practicalities of organics that were the problem but the attitudes of other people: 'One of the great difficulties of converting to organic farming turned out to be convincing others that you had not taken leave of your senses.'

When he first began to run the Highgrove Estate, his intention had been biologically sustainable farming, but from 1986 Charles went even further and set about converting the nine-hundred-acre Home Farm to become wholly organic. Pesticides were banned and visitors were greeted by a large, painted notice announcing: 'Caution. You are entering a GMO-free zone'.

Reflecting back on his suggestion that organic farming might have some benefits and ought to be taken seriously, 'I shall never forget the vehemence of the reaction ... much of it coming from the sort of people who regard agriculture as an industrial process, with production as the sole yardstick of success.'

At the time, people thought he was mad, or at the very least eccentric. But Charles proved his critics wrong and made a great success of the Highgrove Estate, which went on to become something of a role model for sustainable organic farming and enterprise.

The preservation of rare and native breeds has been another source of pride. Charles has successfully raised herds of Tamworth pigs, one of Britain's oldest breeds, Hebridean and Cotswold sheep, and Irish Moiled cows among many other animals. He is said to be particularly fond of his flock of Buff Orpington chickens which were also a favourite with his grandmother, the Queen Mother, and he became patron of the Rare Breeds Survival Trust.

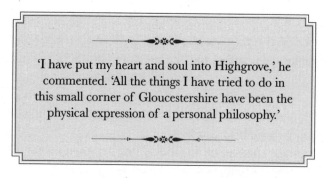

'I have put my heart and soul into Highgrove,' he commented. 'All the things I have tried to do in this small corner of Gloucestershire have been the physical expression of a personal philosophy.'

Decades ahead of most people, Charles made a great success of sustainable farming and business. Describing his practical approach to the royal gardens in his book *The Elements of Organic Gardening*, which he wrote with organic gardener Stephanie Donaldson in 2007, he explained, 'I can only say that for some reason I felt in my bones that if you abuse nature … then she will probably abuse you in return.'

Duchy Originals

In 1990, Charles launched his own brand of organic products, Duchy Originals, named after the Duchy of Cornwall. Initially the brand was an outlet for the organic food grown on the estate but soon expanded into a wide range of products sold throughout the UK and around the world. From 2009, there has been a licensing and distribution agreement with the British supermarket chain, Waitrose, which came to the rescue after the 2008 economic crisis. Renamed Waitrose Duchy Organic, the brand has gone from strength to strength, raising over £30 million for The Prince of Wales' Charitable Fund (now the King Charles III Charitable Fund).

Feeling vindicated in his beliefs, Charles commented, 'The demand for organic food is growing at a remarkable rate. Consumers have made it clear that they want organic produce and every sector of the food chain is responding, with the kind of results we have just seen.'

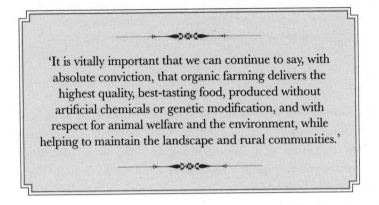

'It is vitally important that we can continue to say, with absolute conviction, that organic farming delivers the highest quality, best-tasting food, produced without artificial chemicals or genetic modification, and with respect for animal welfare and the environment, while helping to maintain the landscape and rural communities.'

Only Connect

For Charles it was always about reconnecting with nature so that everything worked together. He believes fundamentally in the interconnectedness of farming, medicine, architecture, philosophy, spirituality and religion.

In his millennial Reith lecture in 2000 he outlined this integrated approach: 'The idea that the different parts of the natural world are connected through an intricate system of checks and balances which we disturb at our peril is all too easily dismissed ... Only by rediscovering the essential unity and order of the living and spiritual world – as in the case of organic agriculture or integrated medicine or in the way we build – and by bridging the destructive chasm between cynical secularism and the timelessness of traditional religion, will we avoid the disintegration of our overall environment.'

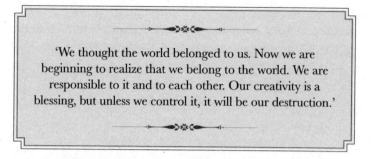

'We thought the world belonged to us. Now we are beginning to realize that we belong to the world. We are responsible to it and to each other. Our creativity is a blessing, but unless we control it, it will be our destruction.'

An advocate of sustainable living for more than forty years now, he is no longer such a lone voice with his comments such as: 'The supporters of organic farming, bio-agriculture, alternative agriculture and optimum production are beginning to make themselves heard.'

'The sustainability revolution will, hopefully, be the third major social and economic turning point in human history, following the Neolithic Revolution – moving from hunter-gathering to farming – and the Industrial Revolution,' he said in a speech in 2009.

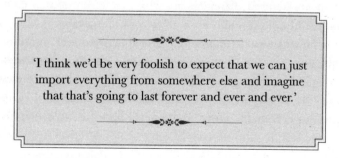

'I think we'd be very foolish to expect that we can just import everything from somewhere else and imagine that that's going to last forever and ever and ever.'

In 2020, Charles announced that he would not be renewing the lease on Home Farm due to his increasing royal duties, but he continues to farm organically at Sandringham. He will also continue to lease Highgrove House as his country home. Control of the estate as part of the Duchy of Cornwall automatically transferred to Prince William when Charles became king.

Practice What You Preach

There is a highly practical side to Charles's desire for sustainable organic living aside from his hands-on approach to gardening and farming. The lighting at Highgrove is partially solar powered, the heating is biomass and pump-fed, and reed bed sewer and composting systems deal with waste. In 2010 he was granted permission to place solar panels on the roof of his London home, Clarence House, and biomass boiler systems have now been installed in all his various homes.

His much-admired Aston Martin DB6, a 21st birthday present from the Queen, has also been given a green makeover. 'My old Aston Martin, which I've had for fifty-one years, runs on – can you believe this – surplus English white wine and whey from the cheese process,' Charles enthused. It's true. The car has been converted to use E85, an eco-fuel composed of 85 per cent bioethanol, made from leftover wine and cheese whey, plus 15 per cent unleaded gas.

COP26

Speaking at the G20 Rome Summit in October 2021, ahead of the United Nations Climate Change Conference, or COP26, Charles described it as the 'last chance saloon' for the planet.

Addressing the audience of world leaders at the opening ceremony of the Conference in Glasgow the following month, he delivered a clear message:

'… the COVID-19 pandemic has shown us just how devastating a global cross border threat can be. Climate change and biodiversity loss are no different. In fact, they pose an even greater existential threat to the extent that we have to put ourselves on what might be called a war-like footing … Time has quite literally run out. The recent IPCC Report gave us a clear diagnosis of the scale of the problem. We know what we must do. With a growing global population creating ever-increasing demand on the planet's finite resources, we have to reduce emissions urgently and take action to tackle the carbon already in the atmosphere, including from coal-fired power stations …'

He called for countries to work together and look to nature to tackle the crisis:

'… After billions of years of evolution, nature is our best teacher … Our efforts cannot be a series of independent initiatives running in parallel. The scale and scope of the threat we face call for a global systems-level solution based on radically transforming our current fossil fuel-based economy to one that is genuinely renewable and sustainable … my plea today is for countries to come together to create the environment that enables every sector of industry to take the action required. We know this will take trillions, not billions of dollars.'

He finished by stressing the need for joint action and cooperation:

> *'Many of your countries are already feeling the devastating impact of climate change through ever-increasing droughts, mudslides, floods, hurricanes, cyclones and wildfires ... Any leader who has had to confront such life-threatening challenges knows that the cost of inaction is far greater than the cost of prevention. So I can only urge you as the world's decision makers to find practical ways of overcoming differences so we can all get down to work together to rescue this precious planet and save the threatened future of our young people.'*

Ever practical, he acknowledged that many countries 'burdened by growing levels of debt, simply cannot afford to go green. Here we need a vast military-style campaign to marshal the strength of the global private sector.'

Charles had previously pointed out that, 'Perhaps it has been too uncomfortable for those with vested interests to acknowledge, but we have spent the best part of the past century enthusiastically testing the world to utter destruction; not looking closely enough at the long-term impact our actions will have.'

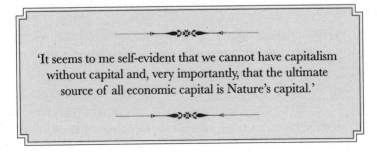

'It seems to me self-evident that we cannot have capitalism without capital and, very importantly, that the ultimate source of all economic capital is Nature's capital.'

In 2022 he again stressed the need for a combined effort to safeguard the future: 'There is an amazing amount that can be done. It is the combined responsibility of all of us – the public sector, the private sector and civil society.'

To the climate change deniers he had this to say, 'It is baffling, I must say, that in our modern world we have such blind trust in science and technology that we all accept what science tells us about everything – until, that is, it comes to climate science.'

Where Are We Now?

Asked for his thoughts on where we stand now, his rather understated view is nevertheless a stark warning, 'I think we're going to find, with climate change and everything else, things like global warming and goodness knows what else and the cost of fuel for a start, that things are going to become very complicated.'

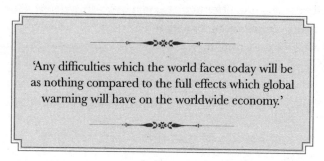

'Any difficulties which the world faces today will be as nothing compared to the full effects which global warming will have on the worldwide economy.'

As King, Charles knows it is no longer possible for him to speak unguardedly on the issues about which he remains passionate but he has found ways to deploy his 'soft power' to greatest effect.

When Liz Truss's short-lived government advised him not to attend the COP27 Climate Conference in Egypt as previously announced, he complied. Instead, he invited international representatives to a reception at Buckingham Palace the evening before it began in November 2022.

On 1 December 2023, King Charles made his first major climate speech as sovereign, addressing world leaders gathered in Dubai at the start of the COP28 UN Climate Summit. His role was ceremonial, but he was attending on behalf of the British government.

He warned that the world was 'dreadfully far off track' and that 'we are seeing alarming tipping points being reached' after a year of record-breaking temperatures across the globe. 'Unless we rapidly repair and restore nature's unique economy, based on harmony and balance, which is our ultimate sustainer, our own economy and survivability will be imperilled.'

He repeated his call for urgent action to tackle the climate crisis, with a stark warning for the future: 'In 2050, our grandchildren won't be asking what we said, they will be living with the consequences of what we did or did not do.'

'I am one of those people who searches. I'm interested in pursuing the path, if I can find it, through the thickets.'

Charles speaking to biographer Jonathan Dimbleby in 1994.

Campaigns

Charles's interest in sustainability and concern about climate change goes beyond farming and conservation to a far broader philanthropy. Among other things, this encompasses an interest in reforestation and soil health, ethical food and fashion, fish stocks and water pollution, poverty and welfare. In 2020 he became a patron of the marine conservation charity Surfers Against Sewage, addressing its conference during the Covid pandemic in June 2021 via video link.

In the decade before he became King, Charles raised around £140 million of donations for more than 400 charities of which he was patron. As Prince of Wales, he remained defiant about his duty to speak out on issues, telling his biographer Jonathan Dimbleby in 1994, 'I don't see why politicians and others should think they have the monopoly of wisdom.'

Perhaps the sheer predictability of his royal role and the restrictions it placed on his life, led him to admit, 'I like to stir things up, to throw a proverbial royal brick through the plate glass of pompous professional pride and jump feet first into the kind of spaghetti bolognaise which clogs this country from one end to the other.' You can sense the frustration of having to stand by and watch while others fail to get things done.

A Force for Change

Talking in 2007 to journalist Robert Hardman in fly-on-the-wall conversations for the BBC documentary *Charles at 60: The Passionate Prince*, he admitted of his campaigning, 'I am a blinding nuisance. You call it meddling, I would call it mobilizing actually.' He explained his approach, 'What I try to do is bring people together and then depart to let them get on with it.'

In the past, Charles has certainly made a habit of challenging the status quo.

In 1986 he was invited to speak to 16,000 alumni at a gala celebrating the 350th Anniversary of Harvard University. In the speech he was funny and self-deprecating, but also serious, addressing matters of education, the environment, and the promotion of human wellbeing – all lifelong concerns of his. His speech received widespread coverage and approval from *The Washington Post* and other sections of the American press, although it was largely ignored at home.

Among his comments were: 'As an old Cambridge man, and one hailing from a college not more than an easy bicycle ride from John Harvard's Emmanuel College, I am particularly pleased and proud to be standing here "in the Yard"… I must confess that I am somewhat surprised as well … because I thought that in Massachusetts they weren't too certain about the supposed benefits of royalty …'

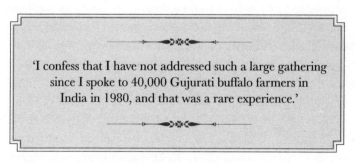

'I confess that I have not addressed such a large gathering since I spoke to 40,000 Gujurati buffalo farmers in India in 1980, and that was a rare experience.'

He went on: 'While we have been right to demand the kind of technical education relevant to the needs of the twentieth century, it would appear that we may have forgotten that when all is said and done, a good man, as the Greeks would say, is a nobler work than a good technologist. We should never lose sight of the fact that to avert disaster, we have not only to teach men to make things, but also to produce people who have complete moral control over the things they make.'

He warned of the need for 'moral and intellectual training if we are to escape from the leadership of clever and unscrupulous men.' Among the challenges facing the world, he suggested, is determining how to 'guard against bigotry, against the insufferable prejudice and suspicion of other men's religions and beliefs, which have so often led to unspeakable horrors throughout human history, and which still do?' He suggested institutions of further education had a vital role to play, 'If they succeed in serving not just the immediate needs of the present but something greater than themselves yet to come, the chances are that they will not only renew themselves but help renew their ailing societies.'

We may have got used to Charles speaking out on the issues about which he feels passionately, but he has admitted that, especially in the early years as Prince of Wales, it wasn't always easy. 'I think people don't quite understand how much it requires to put your head above the parapet. It's no fun having your head shot off all the time.'

Fast Food

Charles's view of fast food is emphatic and damning: 'The price of apparently cheap food is costing nothing less than the Earth!'

He elaborated, 'Fast food may appear to be cheap food and, in the literal sense it often is. But that is because huge social and environmental costs are being excluded from the calculations. Any analysis of the real cost would have to look at such things as the rise in food-borne illnesses, the advent of new pathogens ... antibiotic resistance from the overuse of drugs in animal feed, extensive water pollution from intensive agricultural systems and many other factors. These costs are not reflected in the price of fast food …'

He stressed the negative impact of some modern methods of food production: 'There is a price to be paid at the sharp end … environmentally and everywhere else, for the food that is produced in a particular way.'

There might have been a touch of exasperation when he pointed out: 'What I have been trying to remind people of for the past forty years, is that you can't operate an entire conventional system, whether it's economics, business, or the way we live and surround ourselves, what we eat, without recognizing that there are severe negative externalities that are not being accounted for.'

Slow Food

Alongside Charles's support for organic farming and condemnation of fast food, he has also thought carefully about the impact of meat consumption on the environment, taking the personal decision to reduce the quantity he eats.

Back in 1985 he told reporter Alastair Burnet, 'I actually now don't eat as much meat as I used to. I eat more fish.' More recently he revealed that he makes sure he eats no meat or fish at all for two days a week and no dairy on one day.

Alongside this, he has voiced his appreciation of the slow food movement, and it is easy to see how its values would mesh with his own beliefs. He explained, 'Personally, I have been very impressed by the slow food movement. It is about celebrating the culture of food, of sharing the extraordinary knowledge, developed over millennia, of the traditions involved with quality food production, of the sheer joy and pleasure of consuming food together. Especially within the context of family life, this has to be one of the highest forms of cultural activity.'

Genetically Modified

Given his belief in organic, traditional farming methods, it is no surprise that he has spoken out against the development of genetically modified crops:

'Organic farming has been shown to provide major benefits for wildlife and the wider environment. The best that can be said about genetically engineered crops is that they will now be monitored to see how much damage they cause.'

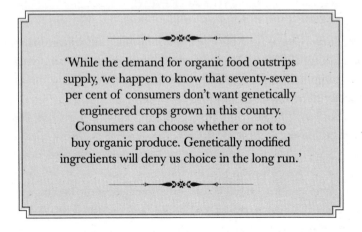

'While the demand for organic food outstrips supply, we happen to know that seventy-seven per cent of consumers don't want genetically engineered crops grown in this country. Consumers can choose whether or not to buy organic produce. Genetically modified ingredients will deny us choice in the long run.'

Delivering the Sir Albert Howard Memorial Lecture in 2008 on genetically modified food, he said:

'For too long we have been conducting a gigantic experiment designed to test nature, and the world, to destruction in order to obtain the empirical evidence that it is possible to do so ... The reason I keep sticking my sixty-year-old head above an increasingly dangerous parapet is not because it is good for my health, but precisely because I believe fundamentally that unless we work with nature in a myriad of ways such as this we will fail to restore the equilibrium we need in order to survive on this planet.'

Fishing

Taught to fish by his mother and father during late summers in Scotland, Charles has been an avid fisherman from an early age, passing on his enthusiasm to his sons and the younger members of the royal family. He has fished around the world but is probably most at home fly fishing on the River Dee in Scotland. On more than one occasion over the years he has been known to extend holidays on the Balmoral estate if the fishing was particularly good.

His interest in fishing as a sport connects with his passion for the environment and fears over the impact of human activity. As long ago as 1969, Charles wrote to then Prime Minister Harold Wilson over his concerns about declining salmon stocks: 'Several species have been wiped out because no one has woken up in time to the danger ... The problem at the moment seems to be if everyone waits for scientific research into salmon netting etc, the stocks will be severely depleted before any regulations are imposed ... When you come up here next weekend I shall attack you on the subject again!'

Evidence gathered by his International Sustainability Unit, which studied fifty sustainably managed fisheries around the world in 2012, suggested that improved management could offer higher profits as well as environmental benefits halting the decline in fish stocks, rather than 'perennially succumbing to the temptation of maximizing short-term income while deferring the costs until later.'

Addressing an audience at Fishmongers' Hall in London, Charles said, 'The story today need no longer be one of doom and gloom and inevitable decline, but one that harbours the possibility of generating more value from a strongly performing natural asset. This potential can only be tapped if we manage it well.'

Charles argued for immediate action to guard against irreversible damage to marine environments and fish stocks. 'Despite the current vulnerable state of global fisheries, if managed properly with a focus on the resilience of the marine ecosystem as a whole, our seas could still provide us with the opportunity to continue harvesting seafood long into the future at similar, or perhaps even higher, volumes than at present.'

The Coronation Food Project

In December 2022 King Charles made a personal donation to a new scheme that aimed to reduce the amount of food waste and tackle problems of food insecurity. The scheme reached its target of £1 million in funding, and distributed eight hundred fridges and freezers throughout the country with the aim of helping food charities save surplus food that would otherwise be wasted.

Increasingly concerned about the impact the cost of living crisis was having on ordinary people, the King built on this scheme and officially launched the Coronation Food Project in November

2023. He wrote: 'Food need is as real and urgent a problem as food waste – and if a way could be found to bridge the gap between them, then it would address two problems in one. To mark my seventy-fifth birthday in this Coronation year, it is my greatest hope that the Coronation Food Project will find practical ways to do just that.'

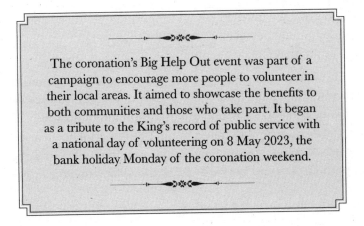

The coronation's Big Help Out event was part of a campaign to encourage more people to volunteer in their local areas. It aimed to showcase the benefits to both communities and those who take part. It began as a tribute to the King's record of public service with a national day of volunteering on 8 May 2023, the bank holiday Monday of the coronation weekend.

Homeopathy and Alternative Medicine

'As soon as the word "holistic" is out of my mouth, I am aware that many people are overcome by a desire to tiptoe to the door and head to the bar to recover,' Charles has commented.

Charles's holistic approach to living extends to an interest in alternative medicine and homeopathy. He first publicly spoke on the subject in 1982, at a dinner celebrating the 150ᵗʰ anniversary of the founding of the British Medical Association, immediately provoking controversy. His speech was seen as deliberately provocative and was criticized by the medical profession as a 'seminal outburst'.

He began:

'I have often thought that one of the less attractive traits of various professional bodies and institutions is the deeply ingrained suspicion and outright hostility which can exist towards anything unorthodox or unconventional … Perhaps we just have to accept it is God's will that the unorthodox individual is doomed to years of frustration, ridicule and failure in order to act out his role in the scheme of things, until his day arrives and mankind is ready to receive his message.'

He continued, 'It is frightening how dependent upon drugs we are all becoming.' Instead, he urged doctors to see 'the patient as a whole human being,' and to rely upon more traditional wisdom to evaluate a person's 'mind, his self-image, his dependence on the physical and social environment, as well as his relation to the cosmos.'

He has continued to write and personally lobby for an integrated health service offering a greater provision of herbal and alternative treatments. He advocated the use of acupuncture, homeopathy, meditation, yoga and massage alongside standard medicines. In his view, 'The whole imposing edifice of modern medicine is like the celebrated tower of Pisa – slightly off balance.'

To this end, Charles launched The Prince's Foundation for Integrated Health in 1993. It closed and was re-launched in 2010 as the College of Medicine, with Charles becoming a patron in 2019. He continues to believe in the importance of a holistic approach to diagnosis and treatment. In 2006 he told the World Health Assembly in Geneva that alternative medicine was 'rooted in ancient traditions that intuitively understood the need to maintain balance and harmony with our minds, bodies and the natural world.'

In May 2022 he recorded a message for 'Wellness After Covid', a virtual healthcare event in which he spoke of the positive effects of yoga in helping to manage stress. He again highlighted the importance of a holistic approach to wellbeing. 'This pandemic has emphasized the importance of preparedness, resilience and the need for an approach which addresses the health and welfare of the whole person as part of society, and which does not merely focus on the symptoms alone.'

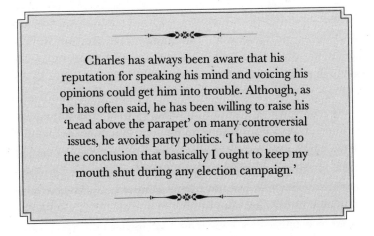

Charles has always been aware that his reputation for speaking his mind and voicing his opinions could get him into trouble. Although, as he has often said, he has been willing to raise his 'head above the parapet' on many controversial issues, he avoids party politics. 'I have come to the conclusion that basically I ought to keep my mouth shut during any election campaign.'

Countryside Agency

Keen to tackle head on some of the problems facing rural communities, beginning in 1999 Prince Charles launched three projects: The Northern Fells Rural Project, YP2-Clay in Cornwall, and Dales Action for Rural Enterprise. In a foreword to a Countryside Agency report in 2003, Charles wrote, 'The people involved in the projects – the community leaders, the rural champions, the volunteers, the mentors, the young people – are the real inspiration. They have shown what can be done and that a noticeable difference can be made. I hope that their achievements will inspire others to follow the example they have set.' He added that the schemes' success had exceeded his expectations.

Rainforests Project

Visiting a rainforest conservation project in Iwokrama, Guyana in 2000, Charles noted, 'The rainforests are the world's thermostat; they sustain the lives of some of the poorest people on earth and yet deforestation continues.' He voiced his belief that the world's wealthy nations should help poorer countries to preserve their rainforests. This was part of the inspiration behind his Prince's Rainforests Project, launched in October 2007. 'My Rainforests Project … has three main elements,' he said. 'Firstly, to determine how much funding the rainforest countries need to re-orientate their economies so that the trees are worth more alive than dead.'

To raise public awareness, Charles, William and Harry, along with a number of celebrities, appeared in a media campaign featuring computer-generated rainforest frogs encouraging people to 'create global determination for change'.

Delivering the Presidential Address in Indonesia in 2008, Charles had pointed out that:

> *'Forests ... are in fact, the world's air-conditioning system – the very lungs of the planet – and help to store the largest body of freshwater on the planet ... essential to produce food for our planet's growing population. The rainforests of the world also provide the livelihoods of more than a billion of the poorest people on this Earth ... In simple terms, the rainforests, which encircle the world, are our very life-support system – and we are on the verge of switching it off.'*

He continued *'... the world is not paying for the services the forests provide. At the moment, they are worth more dead than alive – for soya, for beef, for palm oil and for logging, feeding the demand from other countries ... I think we need to be clear that the drivers of rainforest destruction do not originate in the rainforest nations, but in the more developed countries which, unwittingly or not, have caused climate change.'*

In April 2009, Charles chaired a meeting of fourteen heads of state at which he proposed their governments should offer developing countries economic incentives to preserve forests.

The same year, Charles also addressed business leaders in Rio de Janeiro, ending with the stark warning, 'We only have 100 months to act.'

Carbuncles and Skylines – Architecture that Nourishes the Spirit

Charles has made no secret of his admiration for classical architecture and his despair at contemporary schemes for urban development and modernist buildings. He has famously spoken out, complaining:

'For far too long some planners and architects have consistently ignored the feelings and wishes of the mass of ordinary people in this country. A large number of us have developed a feeling that architects tend to design for the approval of fellow architects and critics – not for the tenants. The same feelings have been shared by disabled people who consider that with a little extra thought, consultation and planning, their already difficult lives could be made less complicated.'

He made the statement during a speech for the 150th anniversary of the Royal Institute of British Architects on 30 May 1984. At the same event he also said of the proposed extension to the National Gallery in Trafalgar Square, London, 'It is like a kind of vast municipal fire station … Like a monstrous carbuncle on the face of a much-loved and elegant friend.' Charles claimed afterwards that he was merely making a personal observation – 'Only after I said it did I begin to appreciate from the response just how many people felt as I did.'

The modernist architect Ludwig Mies van der Rohe's long-delayed plans for an office tower in the Mansion House Square project also came under fire from Charles in the same speech. He declared, 'It would be a tragedy if the character of our capital city were to be further ruined and St Paul's dwarfed by yet another giant glass stump, better suited to downtown Chicago than the City of London.' Neither scheme went ahead.

Along similar lines he compared London's evolving skyline to 'an absurdist picnic table ... We already have a giant gherkin, now it looks as if we are going to have an enormous salt cellar.'

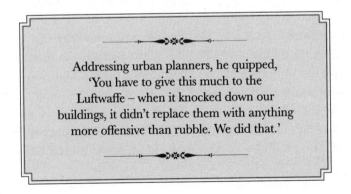

Addressing urban planners, he quipped, 'You have to give this much to the Luftwaffe – when it knocked down our buildings, it didn't replace them with anything more offensive than rubble. We did that.'

A Vision of Britain

The importance of good design goes much deeper than mere aesthetics for Charles. Issues such as 'the environment, architecture, inner-city renewal, and the quality of life' are all inextricably linked. He has long campaigned for local community involvement when it comes to development. In 1988 he wrote and narrated a documentary for the BBC's Omnibus arts series called *HRH Prince of Wales: A Vision of Britain*.

During the film he deplored Birmingham library as, 'A place where books are incinerated, not kept,' and criticized the new British Library in London as looking like 'an assembly hall of an academy for secret police.'

Charles was also dismissive of the proposed Canary Wharf tower. It was designed by architect César Pelli, with construction beginning in 1988. The prince questioned why it needed to be so high (it is now the third tallest building in the UK): 'There is also clearly a certain desire just to be high, so that the building has a certain prominence against the sky.' Charles concluded, 'Maybe it is the sheer height of it. I personally would go mad if I had to work in a building like that. I'd feel "how the hell would you get out in the event of a fire," apart from anything else.'

He has described the cityscape as, 'A jostling scrum of office buildings so mediocre that the only way you ever remember them is by the frustration they induce – like a basketball team standing shoulder to shoulder between you and the Mona Lisa.'

He has also asked, 'Why on earth do we have to be surrounded by buildings that look like machines?' And, 'Why can't we have those curves and arches that express feeling in design? What's wrong with them? Why has everything got to be vertical, straight, unbending, only at right angles – and functional?'

The year after the BBC's Omnibus documentary aired, Charles published a book to delve more deeply into the themes covered in the film. In *A Vision of Britain: A Personal View of Architecture*, he explained his approach as not being anti new development per se. He saw proportion as key: 'Within the basic framework of street widths and building heights there is room for a large range of styles. It is the *scale* which counts.'

Looking at town planning and development, he wrote, 'Anyone can build in a thoroughly unimaginative way. The secret, I believe, lies in creating surroundings which people are attracted to because they have that elusive something extra – what we call character. Apart from anything else, it makes commercial sense. The value of a development is enhanced if you create an attractive environment.'

Later in the book he considered the relation of buildings and landscape and the way in which people relate to their surroundings, 'The trick, it seems to me, is to find ways of enhancing the natural environment, of adding to the sum of human delight by appreciating that man is more, much more, than a mere mechanical object whose sole aim is to produce money. Man is a far more complex creation. Above all, he has a soul, and the soul is irrational, unfathomable, mysterious.'

Throughout, he was careful to emphasize that the views expressed were very much his own and that he did not expect agreement from everyone. But he was keen to show there should not just be one approach and that dialogue was vital. 'My chief object has been to try and create discussion about the design of the built environment; to rekindle an alert awareness of our surroundings; inspire a desire to observe; and, most importantly, challenge the fashionable theories of a professional establishment which has made the layman feel he has no legitimate opinions.'

Poundbury

Following on from the documentary, Charles announced his intention of building a new town within the Duchy of Cornwall near to the town of Dorchester in Dorset.

He explained: 'The holiday traffic pounds through the centre of the town, so they've built, at long last, a ring road. Between the ring road and the town centre there are about 350 acres of Duchy of Cornwall land, into which West Dorset District Council is anxious for the town ultimately to expand. They've asked the Duchy for a long-term development plan.'

The design of the new town, Poundbury, was based on traditional architecture and aimed to provide a mixed-use, integrated community including affordable homes, amenities and businesses alongside open spaces, where people could safely walk rather than relying upon cars.

'The easiest thing for the Duchy would have been to sell the land and leave others to do the development. But I am very keen to try something different,' Charles continued. 'This is a problem facing the whole of southern England – how to build in our countryside without spoiling it.'

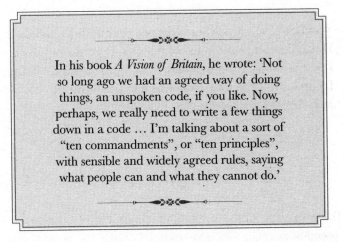

In his book *A Vision of Britain*, he wrote: 'Not so long ago we had an agreed way of doing things, an unspoken code, if you like. Now, perhaps, we really need to write a few things down in a code … I'm talking about a sort of "ten commandments", or "ten principles", with sensible and widely agreed rules, saying what people can and what they cannot do.'

He sought to put this code into practice at Poundbury, working closely with architect and lead planner Léon Krier on the development of the project, which attracted a fair amount of criticism in its early stages. Variously ridiculed as 'a toytown', 'retro-kitsch' and 'a feudal Disneyland', the community is thriving with more than 3,000 inhabitants. It is due for completion in 2025 with an expected population of 6,000.

'When I set out on this venture,' Charles commented, 'I was determined that Poundbury would break the mould of conventional housing development in this country, and create an attractive place for people to live, work and play. Many people said that it could never succeed but I am happy to say that the sceptics were wrong and it is now a thriving urban settlement alongside Dorchester.'

In line with Charles's sustainable eco principles, Poundbury has a full-scale anaerobic digester turning food waste and maize from local farms into renewable energy.

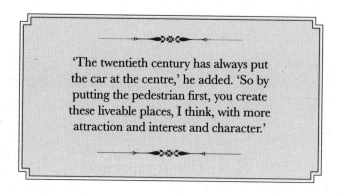

'The twentieth century has always put the car at the centre,' he added. 'So by putting the pedestrian first, you create these liveable places, I think, with more attraction and interest and character.'

Soul Building

As outlined in *A Vision of Britain*, Charles's ideal is 'architecture that nourishes the spirit'. He has very strong views on how that looks and, unsurprisingly, many people, including several architects, disagree with his vision.

In 2007, Charles and his charity The Prince's Foundation intervened to save Dumfries House in Scotland. An eighteenth-century Palladian masterpiece designed by Robert Adam with furniture by Thomas Chippendale and Scottish craftsmen, the interiors and gardens have been comprehensively renovated and restored. It is now a training centre for jobs in heritage, hospitality and gardening. Following this, Charles persuaded the Duchy of Cornwall to buy the Llwynywermod estate in Carmarthenshire, Wales. Architect Craig Hamilton was employed to renovate and add to the property which now includes three rental cottages and a barn as well as the main house for Charles and Camilla. It conforms to Charles's ethos of sustainable living, incorporating locally sourced and recycled materials, a traditional structure and biomass heating system.

The previous year, Charles had revived his interest in Romania, and bought a cottage near the village of Viscri in Zalán Valley, Transylvania. He now owns a cluster of cottages, a farm and manor house nearby.

The Language
of Shakespeare

Speaking at the presentation of the Thomas Cranmer Schools Prize in London in 1989, Charles expressed some horror at the current state of the English language, '[The English] language has ... served as the medium for some of the greatest literature in the world ... Yet a great many people today look in dismay at what is happening to that language ... They wonder what it is about our country and our society ... that we have arrived at such a dismal wasteland of banality, cliché and casual obscenity.'

Society Today

During his years as Prince of Wales, Charles spoke out remarkably candidly on a range of topics, all close to his heart, and about which he cared passionately. He has accepted the criticism this has often provoked as the necessary cost of making his voice heard.

While his title and royal role did not give him any direct powers, he realized early on that he was in a unique position to influence those who did have power to affect change.

He was sometimes despairing of the changes he noted in general attitudes. Writing in 2001 to Lord Irvine, who was Lord Chancellor at the time, he reflected:

'I just wanted to thank you for all your kindness last week in showing me something of your splendid apartments and the wonderful paintings which you have managed to prise out of various collections! It was a delight to see how much care you have taken to restore and respect the very special nature of that part of the Palace of Westminster. I hope you will forgive me if I also take this opportunity to follow up part of [our] discussion … It does seem to me that, over the last few years, we in this country have been sliding inexorably down the slope of ever-increasing, petty-minded litigiousness … I am also struck by the degree to which our lives are becoming ruled by a truly absurd degree of politically correct interference.'

The following year he added, 'The more I have thought about this group of issues, the more convinced I am that we are heading for increasing difficulty … the proliferation of rules and rights makes people over-cautious, stifles initiative and acts as a brake on creative thinking …'

Charles has also been critical of the modern cult of entitlement and the desire to be famous for being famous. In 2003 he wrote an exasperated comment: 'What is wrong with everyone nowadays? Why do they all seem to think they are qualified to do things far beyond their technical capabilities? This is to do with the learning culture in schools as a consequence of a child-centred system which admits no failure. People think they can all be pop stars, high court judges, brilliant TV personalities or infinitely more competent heads of state without ever putting in the necessary work or having natural ability. This is the result of social utopianism which believes humanity can be genetically and socially engineered to contradict the lessons of history …'

'Over the last forty years, the work of my Trust has shown it
is within our power to transform young lives for the better.'

CHARLES SPEAKING IN 2016, ON THE FORTIETH ANNIVERSARY
OF THE FOUNDING OF THE PRINCE'S TRUST.

The King's Trust

Now named The King's Trust, Charles officially launched The Prince's Trust youth charity in 1976, using the £7,500 severance pay he received when he left the Royal Navy, plus other private donations. The core aim has always been to help young people who have faced serious disadvantages in their lives build a better future for themselves. 'In the mid 1970s when I left the Royal

Navy, unemployment in the UK was one of the pressing issues of the time,' Charles explained. 'For young people the problem, as always, was not merely the lack of opportunity represented by joblessness but the feeling that they were being left behind. And it seemed as clear to me then as it does now, that we should do something to try to make a difference, however small. By helping young people find work or training, we hoped that perhaps we would be able to change some individuals' lives for the better.'

The Germ of an Idea

He had begun trialling the idea a couple of years earlier while still in the Navy. A series of pilot projects, creating small enterprises, took place in London, Chester and Cornwall. The plan was to offer grants to young adults looking for 'an adventurous challenge' so they could help themselves and take on 'the responsibility of adulthood'. The focus was always on individuals helping themselves and taking charge.

In a speech to the House of Lords in 1975, Charles outlined the situation as he saw it: 'It seems to me that the problems we suffer in society as a result of violence, mugging and general anti-social behaviour on the part of younger people, are partly due to a lack of outlets into which pent-up energy and frustration and a desire for adventure can be properly channelled.'

The Trust concentrated on young people who had otherwise been written off – those with prison records and drug problems, the homeless and hopeless. It sought to create opportunities and offer a way forward.

'I believe passionately that everyone has a particular God-given ability,' Charles said about the young people who have been helped by his Trust.

He has also declared: 'As human beings, we suffer from an innate tendency to jump to conclusions; to judge people too quickly, and to pronounce them failures or heroes without due consideration of the actual facts and ideals of the period.'

Charles seemed to feel a natural affinity with the young and disillusioned. Perhaps it was because, after university and his naval service, the young Prince of Wales was only too well aware of his own lack of a defined role or fixed purpose in life. Or maybe the germ of the idea came from his beloved grandmother, who had written to him regularly in 1971 while he was serving on board the destroyer HMS *Norfolk* as sub lieutenant. 'Unemployment is very bad and so many boys leaving school can't get jobs. One wishes that one could have a year or even six months of national service of some sort.'

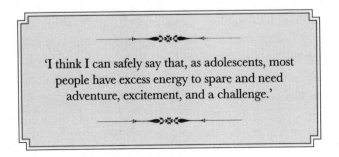

'I think I can safely say that, as adolescents, most people have excess energy to spare and need adventure, excitement, and a challenge.'

Reflecting his own attitude to parenting, his advice to others was, 'If your children want to alter society, listen to their reasons and the idealism behind them. Don't crush them with some clever remark straight away.'

An Adventurous Challenge

The draft deeds for The Prince's Trust were drawn up by the end of 1975, including a logo incorporating Charles's new personal cypher of a 'C' within a crown. In January 1976, Charles explained to somewhat dubious supporters of the scheme: 'The whole point of the exercise is to find challenge and adventure, combined with an element of service, for young people – not going into people's homes for coffee … If we don't insist upon challenge and adventure, to a certain extent, we become like all other voluntary groups and I shall give up at once!'

He reinforced this message at the opening meeting of the Trustees, emphasizing the importance of challenge and adventure, and summing up, 'I established this for a special purpose and to fulfil a need we all agreed was there.'

One of the first beneficiaries was a teenager who was given the money to buy a fishing rod. As a thank you, he later sent Charles a box of flies for salmon fishing that he had made himself.

The acclaimed actor Idris Elba is another of those the Trust helped. It gave him the £1,500 grant he needed to enable him to train as an actor with the National Youth Music Theatre. He had grown up on a council estate in Hackney, North London where gang culture and crime were rife, and he is now one of the charity's goodwill ambassadors, helping to support other youngsters achieve their own potential.

When the Trust launched it struggled to find funding, raising only £7,471 in its first year. Ten years later, in 1986, the sum raised was over £900,000.

From the outset, Charles recognized the importance of making grants available as quickly as possible once a need was established, 'and with a minimum of red tape … to encourage self-help'. He concentrated efforts on those who were alienated and felt let down, taking a chance on young people who were otherwise overlooked. 'Occasionally things will go wrong. Occasionally someone runs off with the money,' Charles accepted. 'Well, that is just one of those things. But they won't all do that. And having taken the risks you find that we'll get enormously beneficial results.'

He stressed this same message in a letter to the then Education Secretary, Kenneth Baker, when The Prince's Trust was working alongside the government's schemes to improve inner cities in the late 1980s. 'I feel very strongly that it is important to turn "poachers into gamekeepers", as it were, and that one should not worry about the past records of such people,' he wrote.

Those who have come to know Charles often say that he always tries to see the best in people. This same principle is at the heart of the Trust – spotting the seed of an idea or ambition in someone and encouraging it to take root and grow.

Interviewed in 2016 by presenters Ant and Dec for an ITV documentary celebrating forty years of The Prince's Trust, Charles spoke at a prison football class, explaining, 'I was always terribly keen we should do as much as possible to reach those who are hardest to reach. A lot of people end up in prison because they haven't had the attention hopefully we can pay to people.'

Asked about the future of the charity in the same documentary, Charles said, 'You can't sit back and think you've done a marvellous job; you need to constantly be thinking of new issues in order to stay relevant.'

Now, more than forty years on from its foundation, the charity has helped over a million young people aged eleven to thirty into education, training and jobs, providing grants and support, and has assisted almost 90,000 young people to start small businesses of their own. In 2015 the Trust began expanding internationally, with bases established in the USA, Canada, Australia and New Zealand.

Although Charles is now King, the work of the Trust carries on as before, with Charles continuing as figurehead. On 10 November 2023, Buckingham Palace announced that The Prince's Trust would be renamed The King's Trust, along with several other charities, that were all founded by Charles while Prince of Wales, taking updated names. These include The Prince of Wales's Charitable Fund, which is now The King Charles III Charitable Fund, and The Prince's Foundation, now known as The King's Foundation.

The revised names reflect the new sovereign's accession speech promise that the 'important work' carried out by the charities would continue 'in the trusted hands of others'.

'The work you do is the rent you pay for
the room you occupy on earth.'

QUEEN ELIZABETH *THE QUEEN MOTHER*.

On Duty

As heir to the throne and Prince of Wales, Charles has been 'on duty' for most of his life. He was just ten when he met his first US president. Dwight D. Eisenhower flew to Scotland in August 1959 to stay as the Queen's guest at Balmoral. Press photos from the visit show a relaxed group gathered on the castle lawns, including Prince Charles and Princess Anne, along with the President, his son

John, the Queen and Prince Philip. Charles would go on to meet all of the following US presidents apart from John F. Kennedy, Lyndon B. Johnson and Gerald Ford.

Heads of State

Fifty-one years later, looking back on his visit with Princess Anne to meet President Nixon in 1970, when Charles gave a speech at the White House, he reflected, 'That was quite amusing, I must say. That was the time when they were trying to marry me off to Tricia Nixon.'

His thank-you note after the trip was more diplomatic: 'The kindness shown to us at the White House was almost overwhelming and for that we are immensely grateful. Both my sister and I take back to Britain the most heartwarming evidence of what is known as the special relationship between our two countries and of the great hospitality shown to us by you and your family.'

Many of Charles's past conversations with US presidents and vice presidents have focussed on his desire to tackle climate change. As King this focus may have to shift.

'As you may possibly have noticed from time to time, I have tended to make a habit of sticking my head above the parapet and generally getting it shot off for pointing out what has always been blindingly obvious to me,' he said in a speech in January 2014.

In the summer of 1988, Charles was increasingly concerned about the situation in Romania and in particular President Ceausescu's environmental policy of 'systemization', which involved the proposed destruction of around 8,000 traditional villages and their replacement with vast agro-industrial centres.

He wrote to the Foreign Secretary, Geoffrey Howe, outlining his concerns:

> *'The point of this letter is really to say that I do believe the situation in Romania should be an urgent priority for the European nations to address. After all, for what did so many of our courageous countrymen die during the last war? Was it merely to see one system of tyranny and misery exchanged for another? … The press is full of Gorbachev and glasnost but they seem to ignore those other parts of Eastern Europe where abominable tyranny still reigns.'*

In April 1989, Charles became one of the first to publicly condemn Nicolae Ceausescu for the 'wholesale destruction of his country's cultural and human heritage', raising the alarm about the proposed destruction of medieval villages. 'The object is to reshape the nation's identity, to create a new type of person, utterly subordinate to its dreams,' Charles claimed. He spoke with the approval of the Foreign Office, having previously condemned the Romanian president's totalitarian regime of oppression five years earlier in a speech delivered in Canada.

Addressing the Bundestag

Charles's first overseas visit as King was to Germany, after the original planned state visit to France had to be postponed because of riots throughout that country in March 2023. Germany was always due to be the second leg of the trip, signalling the importance of both countries – and Europe as a whole – to the UK. This was an important visit at a crucial time, post-Brexit and with war in Ukraine. Former diplomat and ambassador Tom Fletcher explained, 'The monarch is a central part of how the UK projects soft power.'

At the state banquet, Charles pledged to 'strengthen connections' and commented, 'I have been struck by the warmth of the friendship between our nations.' He also focused on environmental sustainability, crediting German expertise in organic farming with 'greatly improving my own farms and soil'.

But it was his historic speech to the Bundestag on 30 March, making him the first British monarch to address the German parliament, that made headlines around the world. He delivered much of it in German and it earned him a standing ovation. 'It means a great deal to both my wife and myself that we have been invited to Germany on my first overseas tour as Sovereign, and it is a particular honour to be here with you where I wish to renew the pledge of friendship between our nations ...' he said.

He went on:

'... Seventy-five years after the Second World War, it was of great importance to me to stand with Germans in honouring all victims of war and tyranny, and to be the first members of my family to participate in those deeply moving commemorations ...

' ...*since I last spoke in this building the scourge of war is back in Europe. The unprovoked invasion of Ukraine has inflicted the most unimaginable suffering on so many innocent people. Countless lives have been destroyed; freedom and human dignity have been trampled in the most brutal way. The security of Europe has been threatened, together with our democratic values.*

'*The world has watched in horror – but we have not stood by. Even as we abhor the appalling scenes of destruction, we can take heart from our unity – in defence of Ukraine, of peace and freedom ....*

'*... Together we must be vigilant against threats to our values and freedoms, and resolute in our determination to confront them. Together we must strive for the security, prosperity and wellbeing that our people deserve.*'

He also took time to touch on other aspects of the relationship between the two countries, acknowledging a 'profound admiration' of one another's literature and music, countryside and art, culture and nightlife. And then there was humour: 'Perhaps most importantly, for the last fifty years we have laughed together – both at each other, and with each other ... In Britain, Germany's comedy ambassador Henning Wehn, has given us an understanding of German quirks, as Monty Python brought our own here. Like all old friends at moments, the warmth of our relationship allows a small smile at each other's expense.'

Entente Cordiale

In June 2020, social distancing rules meant the usual formal handshake greeting was out of the question and so Charles and Camilla greeted President Macron of France with a *Namaste* bow. The President was in the UK to mark the eightieth anniversary of General de Gaulle's broadcast from London to his occupied homeland during the Second World War. President Macron awarded the French Legion d'Honneur to London in thanks for the city's support of the Free French during the war. Charles accepted the order of merit, and, speaking in fluent French, commented on the close connection between the two countries: 'It is a bond forged through common experience sanctified through shared sacrifice and burnished by the deep affection in which we hold each other.'

Charles may not feel that he has the same freedom of expression as sovereign that he did when Prince of Wales, but that did not stop him from again speaking out about climate change during his first state visit to France as King in September 2023.

He made history as the first British sovereign to address both the French Senate and National Assembly. His speech, delivered largely in French, earned him a standing ovation.

Referring to the Entente Cordiale agreement of 1904, which France and the UK signed in order to set aside past rivalries, he said: 'Let us renew it for future generations so that, I would like to propose, it also becomes an agreement for sustainability – in order to tackle the global climate and biodiversity emergency more effectively.'

He also said, 'We must stand together to protect against global warming, climate change and the catastrophic destruction of nature.'

Philosophy and Religion

While in his twenties, Charles's interest in mysticism and personal spirituality was encouraged by his friendship with writer and philosopher Laurens van der Post, who became the prince's spiritual mentor.

'We have lost that sense of meaning within nature's scheme of things which helps to preserve that delicate balance between the world of the instinctive unconscious and that of the conscious,' the prince commented. 'If we did but know it, so many of the things we feel, as it were unconsciously, are things we share, but which seem to become trapped within us through that fear of being thought different or odd.'

He added, 'I rather feel that deep in the soul of mankind there is a reflection as on the surface of a mirror or a mirror-calm lake, of the beauty and harmony of the universe. We must develop an awareness of this to attain inner peace and world peace.'

Satirists have at times had a field day with their image of a young Prince Charles meditating and communing with nature. He has been known to play along with the joke: 'Here I am robed, sandalled, shaven-headed, and with a rather faraway look in my eyes.'

But less amused, he has been forced to firmly deny any dabbling in the occult or with Ouija boards: 'I'm not interested in the occult or any of these things. I'm purely interested in being open-minded.'

Interfaith Initiatives

Charles prides himself on being a freethinker, interested in faith and beliefs in general. His desire to understand other religions has led to criticism, as has his support for interfaith dialogue: 'The future surely lies in rediscovering the universal truths that dwell at the heart of these religions.' He explained to his biographer Jonathan Dimbleby in 1994, 'You find that so much of the wisdom that is represented within these religions coincides.'

He became patron of the Oxford Centre for Islamic Studies after making a speech entitled 'Islam and the West' in which he stated, 'Islam can teach us today a way of understanding and living in the world which Christianity itself is poorer for having lost.'

Expanding on this theme he explained, 'The medieval Islamic world, from Central Asia to the shores of the Atlantic, was a world where scholars and men of learning flourished. But because we have tended to see Islam as the enemy of the West, as an alien culture, society, and system of belief, we have tended to ignore or erase its greatest relevance to our own history.'

Charles pointed out the Islamic contributions to the Western world: 'The surprise … is the extent to which Islam has been a part of Europe for so long, first in Spain, then in the Balkans, and the extent to which it has contributed so much towards the civilizations which we all too often think of, wrongly, as entirely Western.'

And he acknowledged the Golden Age of Islam: 'I think we need to recover the depth, the subtlety, the generosity of imagination, the respect for wisdom that so marked Islam in its great ages.'

He has also said, 'Extremism is no more the monopoly of Islam than it is the monopoly of other religions, including Christianity.' And he claimed, 'Offended by the good relations between faiths and cultures, the extremists seek to break up the communities that make up our modern multicultural society.'

In the aftermath of the July 2005 terrorist bombings in London, Charles wrote an article for the *Mirror* newspaper, calling for tolerance and understanding: 'Britain has the proudest tradition of accommodating new communities. Over recent centuries we have seen how, first Protestants, then Jews, then Muslims, Sikhs and Hindus, have enhanced … the whole of society.'

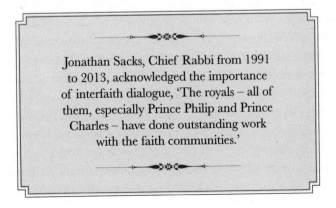

Jonathan Sacks, Chief Rabbi from 1991 to 2013, acknowledged the importance of interfaith dialogue, 'The royals – all of them, especially Prince Philip and Prince Charles – have done outstanding work with the faith communities.'

Charles has made a point of visiting communities of all faiths and attending a range of different religious services and church denominations. He has also taken regular religious retreats in the monasteries of Mount Athos in Greece. His interest in the Orthodox Church is reflected by the Byzantine icons included in his private chapel in the grounds of the Highgrove Estate, and is perhaps unsurprising given his paternal grandmother, Princess Alice of Battenburg, became an Orthodox nun.

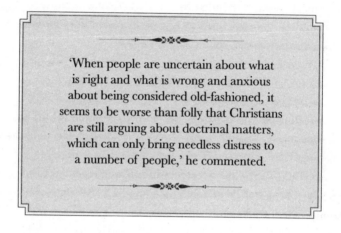

'When people are uncertain about what is right and what is wrong and anxious about being considered old-fashioned, it seems to be worse than folly that Christians are still arguing about doctrinal matters, which can only bring needless distress to a number of people,' he commented.

For Charles, spirituality infuses all parts of life, and care for people, the planet and environment are all interwoven with the sacred. Delivering BBC Radio 4's *Thought for the Day* on 1 January 2000, Charles considered the significance of the new millennium and of rediscovering the notion of hope: 'Hope belongs to a world which recognizes the idea of limits – going with the grain of nature and cherishing and learning from the best of what we have inherited from the past …'

On a sense of wonder, he pointed out:

'In an era when we are tempted to believe that science knows nearly all the answers, it is instructive to recall that Einstein understood the close connection between wonder and the sacred. To him the sense of wonder was the most important sense to open ourselves to the truth, the immensity of the mystery and the divinity of ourselves and our world ...'

He stressed his feelings that:

'In an age of secularism I hope with all my heart that, in the new millennium, we will begin to rediscover a sense of the sacred in all that surrounds us, whether in the way we grow our crops or raise our livestock on the land that God has given us, whether in the way we create places for people to live in the countryside we have inherited, whether in the way we treat disease in our fellow human beings or whether in the way we educate or motivate our young people.'

This echoes the theme of the Reith Lecture that he delivered in 2000 for the BBC, and emphasizes his fundamental belief in the connectivity of all elements of life.

Defender of the Faith and Protector of Faiths

Some thirty years ago, in June 1994, Charles sparked a furore by suggesting he would like to be 'defender of faith' in general rather than 'defender of *the* faith' as his mother and all monarchs since Henry VIII had included in their full regal titles. He posed the idea publicly in the ITV television documentary *Charles: The Private Man, The Public Role*, stating his views clearly:

'I personally would rather see it as defender of faith, not the faith, because it means just one particular interpretation of the Faith, which I think is sometimes something that causes a deal of a problem. It has done for hundreds of years. People have fought each other to the death over these things, which seems to me a peculiar waste of people's energy, when we're all actually aiming for the same ultimate goal, I think. So I would much rather it was seen as defending faith itself which is so often under threat in our day where, you know, the whole concept of faith itself or anything beyond this existence, beyond life itself is considered almost old-fashioned and irrelevant.'

Charles tried to clarify his position on faith in a BBC radio interview in 2015:

'As I tried to describe, I mind about the inclusion of other people's faiths and their freedom to worship in this country. And it's always seemed to me that, while at the same time being defender of the faith, you can also be protector of faiths.' He drew on his mother the Queen's assessment of her role *'not to defend Anglicanism to the exclusion of other religions. Instead, the Church has a duty to protect the free practice of all faiths in this country. I think in that sense she was confirming what I was really trying to say – perhaps not very well – all those years ago.'*

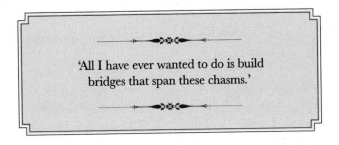

'All I have ever wanted to do is build bridges that span these chasms.'

King and Church

Shortly after the Queen's death, King Charles addressed faith leaders at a reception in Buckingham Palace. He described himself as a 'committed Anglican' but explained that alongside this he felt the monarch had a 'duty to protect the diversity of our country, including by protecting the space for faith itself and its practice through the religions, cultures, traditions and beliefs to which our hearts and minds direct us as individuals.' He also acknowledged those who have no religion, 'By my most profound convictions ... I hold myself bound to respect those who follow other spiritual paths, as well as those who seek to live their lives in accordance with secular ideals.'

In the event, despite speculation that the coronation oath might be altered, at his coronation in Westminster Abbey on 6 May 2023, King Charles III took the titles of defender of the faith and supreme governor of the Church of England. In a deeply religious ceremony, he solemnly promised to: 'maintain the Laws of God and the true profession of the Gospel ... the Protestant Reformed Religion established by law ... the settlement of the Church of England, and the doctrine, worship, discipline, and government thereof, as by law established in England.'

Keep Talking

Charles has a fundamental belief in the need for dialogue and understanding, not just in religion but in every aspect of life. He commented: 'Conflict, of course, comes about because of the misuse of power and the clash of ideals, not to mention the inflammatory activities of unscrupulous and bigoted leaders. But it also arises, tragically, from an inability to understand and from the powerful emotions which, out of misunderstanding, lead to distrust and fear.'

In October 2019, Charles had an audience with Pope Francis at the Vatican. He was there for the ceremony to canonize the nineteenth-century Cardinal John Henry Newman, the first Briton to be made a saint in almost half a century.

Charles praised Cardinal Newman for being 'Able to advocate without accusation, disagree without disrespect and, perhaps most important of all, to see differences as places of encounter rather than exclusion … These are principles that continue to inspire and to guide each new generation.'

The Language of Heaven

When it comes to Anglican church services, like his father Prince Philip, Charles favours the more traditional language of the *Book of Common Prayer* and the older translations of the Bible. 'If English is spoken in heaven … God undoubtedly employs Cranmer as his speechwriter.

The angels of the lesser ministries probably use the language of the *New English Bible* and the *Alternative Service Book* for internal memos.

'*I was totally absorbed. I was in another world, or another dimension; all sense of time evaporated.*'

CHARLES TALKING ABOUT HIS LOVE OF PAINTING.

Off Duty

Five years spent in the Royal Navy, combined with frequent press photographs of him swimming and surfing, on horseback riding to hounds or playing polo, jumping out of aircraft and piloting his own plane, saw Prince Charles's reputation with the public change from that of shy teen to 'Action Man'. Charles disliked the label intensely, along with the playboy image it suggested, but his comments like, 'I believe in living life dangerously,' to a group of journalists also encouraged it.

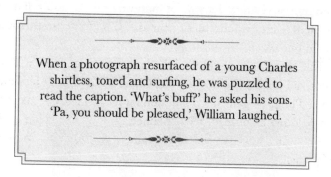

When a photograph resurfaced of a young Charles shirtless, toned and surfing, he was puzzled to read the caption. 'What's buff?' he asked his sons. 'Pa, you should be pleased,' William laughed.

As a young prince, his athletic and physical pursuits were better known than his many cultural interests, probably because they offered greater photo opportunities. He has always been a deep thinker but often struggled to be taken seriously. In the early 1980s, speaking at Cambridge University about religious education and workers' rights, when question time came he was asked, 'Sir, how do you account for your amazing success with women?'

Born to Ride

Like his parents and siblings, Charles learned to ride when he was very young. Naturally cautious, he lacked his sister Princess Anne's easy affinity with horses, but went on to become an accomplished horseman. Along with the Queen, he came to see time out on horseback as offering a sense of freedom and a welcome antidote to the stresses of office: 'If I didn't get the exercise – or have something to take my mind off things – I would go potty.'

He shared his grandmother's enthusiasm for National Hunt steeplechasing, explaining, 'It's a great challenge to try to overcome a certain element of natural fear … going flat out over fences and wondering if you are going to get to the other side in one piece.'

Flat horse-racing, and the five days spent each June at Royal Ascot, did not particularly interest Charles. Along with his father Prince Philip, he gained a reputation for leaving early to take part in a polo match instead. He explained, 'I don't like going to the races to watch horses thundering up and down. I'd rather be riding one myself.'

Prince of Polo

Prince Charles and Princess Anne grew up watching their father play polo at Windsor and it was Prince Philip who bought Charles his first polo pony. He practised playing during school holidays and when he was fifteen, in 1963, he played his first full game in a team captained by his father. From that time onwards, he played regularly with various teams including Cambridge University and the Royal Navy. His two most important professional teams were Maple Leaf and Les Diables Bleus, with which he won the Queen's Cup in 1986. His favoured playing position was as a back and teammates have described him as a great competitor.

On playing polo with his father, Charles said in the 2021 BBC documentary, *Prince Philip: The Royal Family Remembers*, 'I used to enjoy playing polo with him. I used to get endless shouting, "Get up! Stop mucking about!" And I remember playing in a football match, he used to give me instructions … "Get up! Do something!" … He tried to teach me to drive a carriage but that didn't last very long, with him getting more and more annoyed that I wasn't concentrating properly.'

When Charles was first learning to play polo as a teenager, Prince Philip apparently told his coaches, 'Let him have it hot and strong. Be frank and fearless.'

The tough approach clearly didn't put Charles off. And despite numerous falls and broken bones, he has commented more than once, 'I feel a hundred times better after a game of polo.' He also described the sport as 'my one great extravagance.'

From 1992 he played only in charity matches, raising more than £12 million. He made the decision to retire from the game entirely at the end of 2005 after playing for more than forty years. He retains a keen interest in the sport as a spectator, often watching his sons play.

Skiing

Charles learned to ski as a teenager, taking his first lessons in 1963 while staying with Prince Ludwig of Hesse and by Rhine at Tarasp in Switzerland. He became a passionate skier and continued to take annual family skiing holidays, often at Klosters, his favourite resort. There he could ski off-piste and enjoy the silence of the mountains. The week spent there was always an escape, but in March 1988 it also brought tragedy.

The Prince and close friends Charley Palmer-Tomkinson, his

wife Patti and Major Hugh Lindsay set off with guide Bruno Sprecher. They took the lift to the top of the mountain, and were skiing down when they were suddenly overtaken by an avalanche, gigantic slabs of snow crashing towards them. Charles later said, 'I've never forgotten the sound of it, the whole mountain apparently exploding outwards ...' Patti Palmer-Tomkinson was badly injured but Hugh Lindsay was tragically killed.

Greatly shocked by what had happened, flying home the next day, Prince Charles issued a statement clarifying events: '... I would like to emphasize that all the members of my party, including myself, were skiing off the piste at our own risk. We all accepted, and always have done, that the mountains have to be treated with the greatest respect and not treated lightly. There is a special dimension to skiing off the piste which is hard to describe to those who may not have experienced it or may not wish to. My friend, Major Hugh Lindsay, who so tragically died in this appalling accident, shared these feelings to the full, and also understood that there is inevitably a risk involved.'

Earning his Wings

Prince Charles first learned to fly with the Cambridge University Royal Air Force squadron during his second year as a student, and began training as a jet pilot at RAF Cranwell in Lincolnshire in 1971. He made his first solo flight on 31 March 1971 and wrote in his diary for the day, 'The day when I went solo for the first time in the JP [Jet Provost]. Did it after eight hours instead of the normal ten. An exciting feeling to be let loose in my own jet. Convinced I flew it far better without Dick Johns [his flying instructor at the time] in it to criticize my every move … The feeling of power, smooth, unworried power, is incredible.'

Although apprehensive beforehand, the prince discovered he loved flying jets despite finding some of the technical aspects, particularly navigation, difficult. The usual year's training was condensed into five months for him, and he received his wings on 20 August 1971.

Standing on parade for over an hour during the passing out parade at Cranwell was an eye-opening experience and test of endurance, much of the time spent standing rigidly to attention. 'I now know what the poor guardsmen have to go through. I was in agony, my back ached, my knees felt like lead balloons and my feet swelled until I felt my toes were going to pop out of the front of them. However, I avoided fainting and managed to have my wings pinned on my chest without mishap. A marvellous moment.'

That same year, in July, Charles made his first parachute jump, over Studland Bay off the coast of Dorset. There was no question of him allowing nerves to stand in the way of him completing the jump. He noted in his diary:

> *'As I had been clever enough to say I wanted to jump and the press had said I was going to jump I was going to. It was a curious sensation standing in the doorway and just waiting. I was certainly nervous, but I was longing to experience the sensation of launching myself out of the door … I kept having morbid reflections on wrapping myself round the tailplane or hitting my head on the side of the aircraft, or even dropping out of the harness before I reached the water.'*

In fact, when his parachute opened, the prince found himself upside down with his feet caught in the rigging lines. Remaining remarkably calm, he swiftly disentangled himself. 'There was only a short time to admire the view and enjoy the sensation before my feet touched the water and I was trying to get free of the harness.'

Later, with a deserved sense of achievement, he said, 'I've done it … and nobody can take that away from me.'

When Prince Charles was made colonel-in-chief of the Parachute Regiment in 1977, he felt that it was important that he should also complete its parachute training course. For Charles it was simple: 'I felt I should lead from the front or at least be able to do some of the things that one expects others to do … I didn't think I could look them in the eye or indeed ever dream of wearing that beret with the Parachute Regiment badge unless I'd done the course … They all put their hands up in horror – or rather the RAF did – but somehow it was organized and I did it.'

Music

Alongside Prince Charles's action man image, he has always held a deep appreciation for culture and the arts.

It was the Queen Mother who really encouraged the young prince's love of music. When very young, he had been taken to children's concerts at the Royal Festival Hall, but it was a performance by the Bolshoi Ballet at Covent Garden which he watched with his grandmother when he was seven that left a lasting impression. From then on, the pair would regularly attend concerts, ballets and operas together.

Talking to Alan Titchmarsh in a Classic FM radio interview in 2020, Charles said, 'It's so important, I think, for grandparents and other relations to take children at about the age of seven to experience some form of the arts in performance.' He stressed the relevance of music and the arts, 'I've spent a large proportion of my life trying to help them survive or raise money. They are so utterly vital to this country and play such a huge part in culture and diplomacy.'

At prep school he learned the piano and he later took up the trumpet at Gordonstoun. He was modest about his talent for the instrument, remembering, 'I can hear the music teacher now. We would all be playing away and making a hell of a din, and suddenly she couldn't stand it any longer and she would put down her violin and we would all stop and she would shout – she had a heavy German accent and somehow that made her sound more agonized – "Ach! Zoze trumpets! Stawp zoze trumpets!" So I gave up my trumpet.'

He did in fact perform in public at St Giles' Cathedral, Edinburgh with the Gordonstoun school orchestra and also sang the *Messiah* with the choir at Elgin Town Hall, about which he said, 'It was a wonderful thing … and I'm so glad I did it. There were about 150 to 200 people in the chorus and four soloists from London who were very good. It lasts for two and a half hours and it was unbelievably hot; I, as usual, came out looking like a beetroot.'

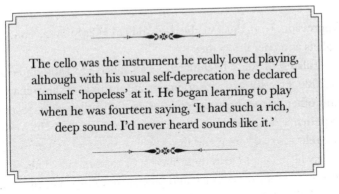

The cello was the instrument he really loved playing, although with his usual self-deprecation he declared himself 'hopeless' at it. He began learning to play when he was fourteen saying, 'It had such a rich, deep sound. I'd never heard sounds like it.'

He recalled studiously practising for a performance with the orchestra of Trinity College Cambridge: 'I loved playing in the orchestra at Trinity – albeit rather badly. I remember playing in Beethoven's Fifth Symphony and trying to practise in my room at Cambridge to an old record conducted by Herbert von Karajan, who was the great conductor in those days, in the sixties. There was me sitting with my cello and my tuning fork, and I put this thing on, and of course he took it at an incredible lick – you've no idea how fast!'

He said of playing an instrument, 'It anchors you and connects you. It's a useful antidote to sitting in front of a screen every day.' And he especially valued his times playing as part of an orchestra: 'I find the whole experience of being with the orchestra or listening to it in a wonderful great hall, I mean it is extraordinary because the sound completely surrounds you and there is nothing to substitute for that I think. It's that wonderful sensation of being part of an immense whole.'

As King, Charles still finds music a real respite and frequently listens to favourite pieces while working.

Art and Painting

In his book, *A Vision of Britain*, Charles reflected, 'Drawing makes you *look* at the world, to visualize clearly what you see and what you propose to design. No amount of computers can substitute for that.'

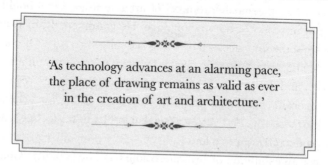

'As technology advances at an alarming pace, the place of drawing remains as valid as ever in the creation of art and architecture.'

Charles always thought the photographs he took were 'rather flat' and delivered a result 'which is probably almost identical to somebody else's photographs.' It was this desire to create 'his own individual interpretation', for a more personal record of what he saw, that drew him to take up painting more seriously in his early twenties. His father encouraged this interest, although his own preference was for oils while Charles always favoured watercolours. He liked their immediacy that 'gives no time for second thoughts. It comes off or it does not, but the excitement of the attempt is to the performer truly electric.' He particularly enjoys painting landscapes outdoors, really looking and noting 'the quality of light and shade, of tone and texture, and of the shape of buildings in relation to the landscape.'

In 1987, one of his paintings was chosen to be included in the Royal Academy's Summer Exhibition having been submitted anonymously.

Charles is a passionate promoter of art as a subject that should be taught in schools from a young age. He commented, 'In Britain we are sometimes accused of being "visually illiterate". Of course we're not, but we do now need a far greater emphasis on art and design and drawing skills in our schools, so that they are regarded as important, not "weak" subjects. You can't start teaching children to draw too soon. If we *are* a nation that lost its ability to "see", then we paid a terrible price for it.'

For an exhibition of his watercolours at The Garrison Chapel in London in 2022, Charles wrote, 'Painting transports me into another dimension which, quite literally, refreshes parts of the soul which other activities can't reach.'

After a satisfying day painting outdoors, he reflected, 'This was one of those special occasions when I could actually feel the inner appreciation of the beauty of the moment passing like an electric current through the brush in my hand.'

In some ways it became almost a form of meditation for him, seeing his art as, 'A part of you that's still there, while the rest of you is gone.'

All the World's a Stage

In an interview with television presenter Cliff Michelmore before his investiture as Prince of Wales in 1969, Charles spoke enthusiastically about acting, admitting that if he hadn't been royal he would have considered becoming an actor. 'It's great fun. I love doing it. Whether I could do it professionally is another matter. It gives me great pleasure.'

He had acted at Gordonstoun; his first role was the Duke of Exeter in Shakespeare's *Henry V*, which he said gave him, 'One rather splendid speech at the French court.' He then played the lead in *Macbeth* when he was seventeen, and was a member of the Dryden Society at Trinity College Cambridge, where he appeared in a number of comic roles.

Along with the rest of his family, Charles famously enjoys playing games of charades, often at Sandringham or Balmoral: 'It's the greatest possible fun. I love it.' And like his mother, he is said to be a good mimic.

Off the Cuff

Charles has frequently credited his ability to get on with the job in hand, no matter what, to his sense of humour.

His comments on that include: 'Were it not for my ability to see the funny side of my life, I would have been committed to an institution long ago.'

And, 'As long as I do not take myself too seriously, I should not be too badly off.'

In a similar vein, when asked by broadcaster and journalist,

David Frost, how he would describe himself, Charles quipped, 'Sometimes as a bit of a twit.'

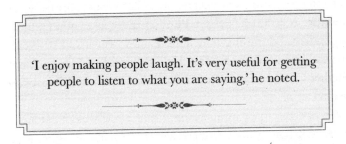

'I enjoy making people laugh. It's very useful for getting people to listen to what you are saying,' he noted.

Feeling cheerful as he left London's King Edward VII hospital after a hernia operation in March 2003, Charles couldn't help himself joking, 'Hernia today, gone tomorrow.'

Reflecting his general philosophy on life, he said, 'Humility is to make a right estimate of one's self. It is no humility for a man to think less of himself than he ought, though it might rather puzzle him to do that.'

In a less than diplomatic letter about the annual Turner Prize for art, Charles wrote to Kim Howells, then a junior minister at the Department for Culture, Media and Sport, 'It's good to hear your refreshing common sense about the dreaded Turner prize. It has contaminated the art establishment for so long.' In 2002 Howells had described the prize as 'conceptual bullshit'.

The Prince and the Press

Over the years as Prince of Wales, Charles often referred to his misrepresentation by the press and at times he clearly felt totally misunderstood.

'Awkward, cantankerous, cynical, bloody-minded, at times intrusive, at times inaccurate and at times deeply unfair and harmful to individuals and to institutions,' was his damning verdict on parts of the media.

During one royal engagement, he turned to waiting journalists and snapped, 'Have any of you the slightest idea what I'm doing here?'

Taking a more measured view of the media, he said, 'As I get older, I find less privacy becomes available and more people seem to be interested in every small and minute aspect of one's life. Somehow you have to have the outlook or philosophy which enables you to bear it, otherwise, I promise you, it's very easy to go mad.'

Looking at things from a newspaperman's point of view, he added, 'He's got a job to do – I've got a job to do. At times they happen to coincide, and compromise must occur, otherwise misery can so easily ensue. I try to put myself in their shoes, and I hope they try to put themselves in mine, although I appreciate that is difficult.'

However, he has also joked, 'It's when nobody wants to write about you or take photographs of you that you ought to worry in my sort of job.'

Best-Dressed

On being told he had been named 'Best-Dressed Man in the World' by *Esquire* magazine in 2009, the prince was typically understated:

'I have lurched from being the best-dressed man to being the worst-dressed man. Meanwhile, I have gone on – like a stopped clock – and my time comes around every twenty-five years.'

He has also been brutally self-deprecating about his physical appearance, saying, 'I've got a long body and short legs. And please don't blame photographers for making my ears look large. They are large.'

He was underestimating his sartorial flair, making number six in *GQ* magazine's Top Ten Best-Dressed Men list in 2019 as well regularly featuring in a number of other such lists. His classic style and attention to detail are noted as marking him out as a style icon, beating off competition from younger Hollywood idols.

*'I always like the term "family circle". It
sounds so close, and safe and happy.'*

QUEEN ELIZABETH THE QUEEN MOTHER SPEAKING IN 1930 AFTER
THE BIRTH OF HER SECOND DAUGHTER, PRINCESS MARGARET ROSE.

Family and Friendship

The royal family is like no other – undoubtedly born to huge wealth and privilege, but this comes with an equal weight of responsibility and duty. Members are destined to live always in the public eye, every move and relationship scrutinized, every utterance and appearance analysed and judged. It is not surprising that Prince Philip reckoned, 'The children soon discover that it's much safer to unburden yourself to a member of the family rather than just a friend … You see, you're never quite sure … a small indiscretion can lead to all sorts of difficulties.'

Son and Heir

'Relationships with fathers can be such complex ones. So often, I suppose, one must long to have got on better or to have been able to talk freely about the things that matter deeply but one was too inhibited to discuss,' Charles reflected.

In his 1969 interview for the BBC, Charles said his father 'had a strong influence on me.' He continued, 'My father has been a great help; he lets one get on with it and gives you the opportunity to get on with it. He has been a moderating influence and an influence of great wisdom.'

At the same time, he said of his mother, 'I tend to think of her as a marvellous person and a wonderful mother. I think of my family as very special people. The Queen has a marvellous sense of humour and is terribly sensible and wise.'

When Charles was born, his mother was still Princess Elizabeth and was determined to be involved with her baby's care as an active mother, rather than hand him over to nurses to look after. But any idea of a normal family life vanished four years later with the sudden death of her father King George VI and her ascension to the throne aged just twenty-five. As Queen Elizabeth, she faced an overwhelming challenge and a daunting workload.

Speaking as an adult, Charles remembered her appearing at bathtime wearing the heavy St Edward's Crown, practising for her coronation. She and Prince Philip taught Charles and Anne to ride horses, but the parents mainly saw the children after breakfast or tea and occasionally at bedtime. 'Mummy was a remote and glamorous figure who came to kiss you goodnight, smelling of lavender and dressed for dinner.'

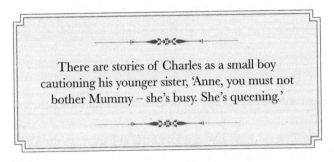

There are stories of Charles as a small boy cautioning his younger sister, 'Anne, you must not bother Mummy – she's busy. She's queening.'

In domestic family matters, the Queen decided early on to defer to Prince Philip who could be a hard taskmaster, especially where his gentle, rather dreamy eldest son was concerned. Philip found Anne's tougher character easier to understand.

In the posthumous BBC documentary, *Prince Philip: The Royal Family Remembers*, Charles reflected, 'You certainly wanted to please my father when given instructions.'

He may not have wanted to disappoint Prince Philip but that could also encourage his competitive side. After he learned to ski, he was quick to tell his father, who had never really taken to the slopes, 'I've got one sport you haven't now.'

Acknowledging the sometimes prickly relationship with his

eldest son, Prince Philip commented, 'He's a romantic and I'm a pragmatist. That means we do see things differently ... And because I don't see things as a romantic would, I'm unfeeling.' He also alluded to Charles's empathy for others, 'He has no interest in things, but all the more for persons.'

In his biography *The Prince of Wales*, Jonathan Dimbleby includes Charles's letter of condolence to his good friend Nicholas Soames after the death of his father, Lord Soames, in 1987. The letter gives an insight into Charles's own feelings about his relationship with Prince Philip at the time. Charles wrote: 'Relationships with fathers can be such complex ones ... but that difficulty pales into insignificance when faced with the fact that a very important figure in one's life is no longer going to be there but is embarking on a mysterious journey into a new and more glorious dimension.'

My Dear Papa

Despite their different personalities, father and son shared many of the same interests and core values. They had clashed over the years, but there was no doubting their mutual respect and love for one another. As both mellowed, they found much to agree upon. Media correspondent Robert Jobson, who specializes in covering the royal family, quotes a source close to the royal household who explained, 'They shared common ground on the future direction of the monarchy, on religious issues – even on the environment. They both believed in interfaith dialogue and that talking openly and honestly can only help strengthen communities and understanding.'

The day after Prince Philip's death at Windsor Castle on 9 April 2021, Charles paid a moving televised tribute to his 'dear Papa':

'I particularly wanted to say that my father, for I suppose the last seventy years, has given the most remarkable, devoted service to the Queen, to my family and to the country, but also to the whole of the Commonwealth.'

He mentioned that he was moved by the public sympathy for the family's loss: 'My dear Papa was a very special person who I think above all else would have been amazed by the reaction and the touching things that have been said about him, and from that point of view we are, my family, deeply grateful for all that. It will sustain us in this particular loss and at this particularly sad time. Thank you.'

A Duchy Original

When Charles turned seventy on 14 November 2018, the Queen hosted a formal dinner at Buckingham Palace to celebrate the occasion at which she gave a moving tribute to her son, speaking as both sovereign and mother:

'It is a privilege for any mother to be able to propose a toast to her son on his seventieth birthday ... My mother saw me turn seventy, of course, and she was heard to observe that seventy is exactly the age when the number of candles on your cake finally exceeds the amount of breath you have to blow them out. Over his seventy years, Philip and I have seen Charles become a champion of conservation and the arts, a great charitable leader – a dedicated and respected heir to the throne to stand comparison with any in history – and a wonderful father.

'Most of all, sustained by his wife Camilla, he is his own man, passionate and creative. So, this toast is to wish a happy birthday to my son, in every respect a duchy original.'

Among the most touching scenes in the 2016 BBC television documentary programme *Elizabeth at 90 – A Family Tribute*, were those showing Charles and his mother reminiscing and laughing together. The warmth of their relationship shone through.

During Queen Elizabeth II's Platinum Jubilee celebrations in 2022, which marked the seventieth anniversary of her accession to the throne, in February the Queen expressed her 'sincere wish' that Camilla would become queen consort when Charles became king, making her support for Queen Camilla unambiguous. It also sent a clear signal of her confidence in her son as future monarch. At the time, a spokesperson said the couple was 'touched and honoured' by this declaration.

Your Majesty, Mummy

During the BBC's *Platinum Party at the Palace*, in June, Charles paid his own highly personal tribute, beginning his address to his mother, 'Your Majesty, Mummy.' He continued, 'You have met us and talked with us. You laugh and cry with us and, most importantly, you have been there for us, for these seventy years. You pledged to serve your whole life – you continue to deliver. You continue to make history.' In a poignant reference to his father's absence and the fact that this was the first major milestone for the Queen without the support of her husband, Charles added that Her Majesty's 'strength and stay' Prince Philip is 'much missed this evening but I am sure he is here in spirit. My papa would have enjoyed the show and joined us wholeheartedly in celebrating all you continue to do for your country and your people.'

After Queen Elizabeth II's death just a few weeks later on 8 September 2022, Charles made his first televised address as King, delivering a moving and heartfelt tribute to his 'darling mama':

'I speak to you today with feelings of profound sorrow. Throughout her life, Her Majesty the Queen – my beloved mother – was an inspiration and example to me and to all my family, and we owe her the most heartfelt debt any family can owe to their mother; for her love, affection, guidance, understanding and example. Queen Elizabeth's was a long life, well lived; a promise with destiny kept and she is mourned most deeply in her passing. That promise of lifelong service I renew to you all today.'

Expressing his gratitude towards his mother, he said, 'To my darling mama, as you begin your last great journey to join my dear late papa, I want simply to say this: thank you. Thank you for your love and devotion to our family and to the family of nations you have served so diligently all these years. May "flights of angels sing thee to thy rest".'

There was no doubting the genuine affection Charles felt for both his parents. This was clearly evident in his moving words at their funerals and again in his very obvious emotion when unveiling life-size bronze statues of the late Queen and Prince Philip at the Royal Albert Hall on 11 November 2023 during a special Festival of Remembrance.

The Most Magical Grandmother

Charles always had an exceptionally close bond with his grandmother. She provided the young prince with the warmth and affection he craved while his parents were occupied with royal duties and frequently away on official overseas visits.

As a child, he saw her regularly at Royal Lodge, her home in Windsor Great Park. 'Ever since I can remember, my grandmother has been a most wonderful example of fun, laughter and warmth, and above all, exquisite taste in so many things,' he wrote. 'For me she has always been one of those extraordinary, rare people whose touch can turn everything into gold ... She belongs to the priceless brand of human beings whose greatest gift is to enhance life for others through her own effervescent enthusiasm for life.'

Watching his mother crowned Queen on 2 June 1953 amid great pomp and ceremony, four-year-old Prince Charles was encouraged by his grandmother: 'Try and remember this.'

Quite simply, she was for him, 'The most magical grandmother you could possibly have.' For the Queen Mother, widowed at the early age of fifty-one, time spent with her grandchildren Charles and Anne provided her 'only happiness'. She always encouraged her sensitive grandson and in one letter wrote to him, 'You have made your desiccated old grandmother laugh immoderately, and long may you continue to do so.'

The young prince's letters to her reflect the closeness of their relationship. On 12 July 1959, while a pupil at Cheam School, he wrote, 'Dear Granny, I do hope you are well and having a lovely time ... We played a match yesterday against Cothill, in which I made one. The under XI lost though, but the first XI won! I got a letter from Mummy and Papa last week, they said it was very hot ... with lots and lots of love from your loving grandson, Charles.'

The Queen Mother shared with him her love of music and culture, along with her delight in travel and fascination with the architecture and art of Renaissance Italy. Charles has frequently acknowledged her profound influence on him and it is no surprise that his book, *A Vision of Britain: A Personal View of Architecture*, has the dedication: 'This book is dedicated to my grandmother, who always encouraged me to look and to observe'.

After her death on 30 March 2002, aged 101, Charles said, 'I miss my grandmother every day. I miss her vitality, her interest in the lives of others, her courage and determination, her perceptive wisdom, her calm in the face of all difficulties, her steadfast belief in the British people and above all her unstoppable sense of mischievous humour.'

Royal Romance

Aside from the many rumoured romances, Charles's genuine relationships were always discreet. However, as he commented more than once, he only had to be seen speaking to a girl for it to be assumed they were dating: 'I've only got to look twice at someone and the next morning I'm engaged to her.' And every time a name was added to the list, the media would go into overdrive assessing every aspect of the supposed new girlfriend and her potential as a future royal bride.

In matters of the heart, he was thoughtful but maybe not always wise. Questioned about his views on marriage, as he often was, Prince Charles said in an interview with journalist Kenneth Harris, writing for the *Observer* in June 1974:

'I'd want to marry someone whose interests I could share. A woman not only marries a man, she marries into a way of life – a job, into a life in which she's got a contribution to make. She's got to have some knowledge of it, some sense of it, or she wouldn't have a clue about whether she's going to like it. And if she didn't have a clue, it would be risky for her, wouldn't it? If I'm deciding on whom I want to live with for fifty years – well, that's the last decision on which I would want my head to be ruled entirely by my heart.'

In an earlier BBC interview with television presenter Cliff Michelmore, Charles outlined the difficulties, as heir to the throne, of choosing a marriage partner. 'When you marry in my position you are going to marry someone who will become queen. And you've got to choose somebody very carefully who can fulfil this particular role. It has got to be someone pretty special. The one advantage of marrying a princess is that they do know what happens. The only trouble is I'd like to marry somebody English, or British.'

In his twenties and heir to the throne, Prince Charles was considered one of the world's most eligible bachelors. Nicknamed 'Action Man' by the press, he was depicted as something of a daredevil, frequently photographed parachuting, surfing, playing polo and riding with the hunt.

In March 1975, he said, 'I have read so many reports recently telling everyone who I am about to marry that when last year a certain young lady was staying at Sandringham a crowd of about ten thousand appeared when we went to church. Such was the obvious conviction that what they had read was true that I almost felt I had better espouse myself at once so as not to disappoint too many people.' On this occasion it is assumed that he was speaking about Laura Jo Watkins, the daughter of an American admiral. Charles had met her in California in March 1974, but, as a Catholic, she was at the time barred from marrying the heir to the British throne.

Charles was well aware that not everyone's apparent interest in him was genuine. 'Various professional ladies hurl themselves without warning against one's person while one is emerging innocently from boiling surf or having executed a turn on a ski slope. All this may be harmless publicity and good for the ladies' careers, but what do you think it does to my ego?'

He knew that the press for their part had an unending appetite for such images: 'All the newspapers seem to be interested in are pictures of me falling off a horse or having a girl fling her arms around my neck. You'd think it was the only thing I ever did.'

Whatever 'In Love' Means

Interviewed shortly after the announcement of his engagement to Lady Diana Spencer on 24 February 1981, the couple were asked if they were in love. Diana answered instantly, 'Of course.' Prince Charles's now infamous response was, 'Whatever "in love" means.' Interviewed years later, after their separation, Princess Diana admitted this reply, 'Threw me completely … Absolutely traumatized me.'

Charles proposed to Diana at the start of February just before she left for a holiday in Australia with her mother and stepfather. He explained, 'I wanted to give her a chance to think about it – to think if it was all going to be too awful.'

Widely described as 'the wedding of the century' and a 'fairytale', Charles and Diana were married on 29 July 1981 at St Paul's Cathedral. The couple were greeted by cheering crowds and it is estimated that 750 million people watched worldwide. During the ceremony, Diana repeated the names of her husband-to-be in the wrong order – 'Philip Charles Arthur George' which was her new father-in-law's name. Charles also muddled his vows, leaving out 'worldly' and promising instead to share all Diana's goods with her, at which point Princess Anne joked, '*That* was no mistake!'

Charles wrote about the day: 'What an unbelievable day it was – that went far too quickly. I couldn't somehow savour all I wanted to savour and I was totally overwhelmed and overcome by the way in which the whole country seemed to have been a favourite guest at the wedding, right down to the way everyone cheered when we said "I will" etc … It was one of the most moving experiences I've ever known.'

Rumours of problems between the couple began circulating early on in their marriage. After a two-week honeymoon cruise on board the royal yacht *Britannia*, Charles and Diana went to stay at

Balmoral. Their differences were already showing. Diana became increasingly moody and withdrawn, very different from the happy, easy-going young woman she had seemed. Jonathan Dimbleby quotes a confidential letter the prince wrote from the yacht, 'Diana dashes about chatting up all the sailors and the cooks in the galley etc, while I remain hermit-like on the verandah deck, sunk with pure joy into one of Laurens van der Post's books.'

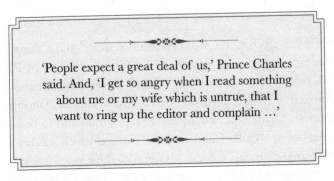

'People expect a great deal of us,' Prince Charles said. And, 'I get so angry when I read something about me or my wife which is untrue, that I want to ring up the editor and complain ...'

Writing to a relative in 1983 about his fears for Diana on their royal tour of Australia and New Zealand, he said, 'The crowds which have turned out to see her – and assault her with flowers – have been enormous by Australian standards. Officials say they are the biggest since my mama came in 1954 ... I worry so much about what I have landed her in at such an impressionable age – the intensity of interest must be terrifying for her.'

Five years into their marriage there was no hiding the distance between the couple, and the tabloid newspapers became frenzied in their interest in the situation. Charles's public role and charitable work was largely ignored amid the speculation about the 'warring Waleses', and he worried about the damaging effect the focus on their disintegrating relationship would have on the monarchy: 'That is the total agony about the situation and I don't see how much longer one can go on trying to sweep it under the carpet and pretend nothing is wrong.'

Charles and Diana formally separated in December 1992, towards the end of the Queen's infamous *annus horribilis*. Early in the year Princess Anne and Captain Mark Phillips divorced, while the Duke and Duchess of York separated. Princess Diana was photographed looking sad and lonely sitting in front of the Taj Mahal, the famed monument to love and marriage. The summer brought further disclosures with the publication of Andrew Morton's book about the princess. Embarrassment continued for the palace when the *Sun* newspaper printed the transcript of the so-called 'Squidgygate' tapes of an intimate phone call between Diana and James Gilbey.

Two years later, Charles agreed to take part in a television documentary, *Charles: The Private Man, the Public Role,* marking twenty-five years since his investiture as Prince of Wales. It is largely remembered for his interview with Jonathan Dimbleby on the breakdown of his marriage to Princess Diana and his public admission that he had been unfaithful to her.

Questioned about infidelity he admitted he had been, 'Faithful and honourable until it became irretrievably broken down, us both having tried.'

'My Darling Wife'

'All my life, people have been telling me what to do. I'm tired of it,' Charles told BBC journalist Gavin Hewitt in 1998 when asked about his relationship with Camilla. 'My private life has become an industry. People are making money out of it. I just want some peace.'

By 2005, it was clear to all that Camilla was the love of Charles's life and his chosen companion. In February, Clarence House issued a formal statement confirming the couple were to marry: 'It is with great pleasure that the marriage of HRH the Prince of Wales and Camilla Parker Bowles is announced. It will take place on Friday 8 April.' The wedding was delayed by a day to allow Charles to represent the Queen at the funeral of Pope John Paul II in Vatican City.

Appearing relaxed but also playing down the significance of his upcoming second marriage, Charles described Camilla and himself as, 'Just a couple of middle-aged people getting wed.'

The marriage took place at the Guildhall in Windsor at 12.30 p.m. with the couple's sons Prince William and Tom Parker Bowles acting as witnesses. In keeping with royal tradition, the wedding rings were made from 22 carat Welsh gold.

The civil ceremony was followed by a Service of Prayer and Dedication held that afternoon in St George's Chapel, Windsor Castle. Eight hundred guests attended the televised ceremony, including the Queen and Prince Philip. Led by the then Archbishop of Canterbury Rowan Williams, Charles and Camilla joined the congregation in reading a prayer which is considered to be the strongest act of penitence in the Anglican Church. It was written by Thomas Cranmer, Archbishop of Canterbury under King Henry VIII. It was widely reported in the media afterwards and generally viewed as a confession of past sins: 'We acknowledge and bewail our manifold sins and wickedness, which we, from time to time, most grievously have committed, by thought, word, and deed, against thy divine Majesty, provoking most justly thy wrath and indignation against us. We do earnestly repent, and are heartily sorry for these misdoings.'

At the time there was some press speculation that the Queen and Prince Philip did not attend the civil ceremony because they disapproved of the marriage. In reality, it was a reflection of the Queen's constitutional position and traditional faith. Her genuine happiness at the occasion was apparent in her warm speech later that day, complete with racing theme (the Grand National was taking place the same day). She toasted Charles and Camilla saying, 'They have overcome Becher's Brook and The Chair [references to the Grand National's most challenging fences] and all kinds of other terrible obstacles. They have come through and I'm very proud and wish them well. My son is home and dry with the woman he loves … [welcome] to the winner's enclosure.'

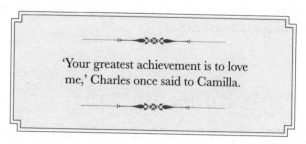

'Your greatest achievement is to love me,' Charles once said to Camilla.

Speaking just before their tenth wedding anniversary in 2015, Charles paid tribute to his wife, 'It's always nice to have somebody on your side … She is an enormous support. The great thing is we laugh a lot because she sees the funny side of life, thank God.'

When asked during the documentary *Prince, Son and Heir: Charles at 70* if she thought her husband's future role as King weighed heavily upon him, Camilla replied firmly, 'No, I don't. I think his destiny will come, he's always known it's going to come, and I don't think it does weigh on his shoulders at all. It's just something that's going to happen.'

In his first address to the country as King, Charles paid tribute to his mother's dedication but also spoke of his wife, acknowledging the vital role she played: 'This is also a time of change for my family. I count on the loving help of my darling wife, Camilla. In recognition of her own loyal public service since our marriage seventeen years ago, she becomes my Queen Consort. I know she will bring to the demands of her new role the steadfast devotion to duty on which I have come to rely so much.'

Father and Sons

When Prince William was born on 21 June 1982, Charles was every bit the doting father. The next day, he emerged first from St Mary's Hospital, Paddington cradling his tiny son. 'Isn't he the most beautiful baby you ever saw?' he said.

Writing to his second cousin Patricia Mountbatten, Charles's joy at becoming a father was evident: 'The arrival of our small son has been an astonishing experience and one that has meant more to me than I ever could have imagined. I am so thankful I was beside Diana's bedside the whole time, because I felt as though I'd shared deeply in the process of birth and as a result was rewarded by seeing a small creature who belonged to us, even though he seemed to belong to everyone else as well.'

After Prince Harry's birth in 1984, Prince Charles commented that his new baby son was, 'Extraordinarily good, sleeps marvellously and eats well.' He also thought he was 'the one with the gentle nature' by comparison with his elder brother Prince William, who was by then a boisterous two-year-old toddler.

Asked what character traits he hoped his sons would develop, Charles answered, 'Sensitivity to others, which by any definition is actually called good manners ... and also, on the whole, do unto others as you'd have them do unto you, which is not a bad way of trying to operate.'

His eldest son Prince William has said of his father, 'He has amazing personal discipline. So, he has – and it's frustrated me in the past a lot – he has a routine. The only way to fit all this stuff in is things have to be compartmentalized. The man never stops. I mean, when we were kids, there were bags and bags and bags of work that the office just sent to him. We could barely even get to his desk to say goodnight to him.'

Prince Harry also remembered his father working hard long hours late into the evening. He commented, 'Countless times, late at night, Willy and I would find him at his desk amid mountains of bulging blue post bags – his correspondence. More than once I discovered him, face on the desk, fast asleep. We'd shake his shoulders and up he'd bob, a piece of paper stuck to his forehead.'

Twenty-four hours after he became King, Charles made his first public address on 9 September 2022 and spoke about both his sons:

'As my Heir, William now assumes the Scottish titles which have meant so much to me. He succeeds me as Duke of Cornwall and takes on the responsibilities for the Duchy of Cornwall which I have undertaken for more than five decades. Today, I am proud to create him Prince of Wales, Tywysog Cymru … With Catherine beside him, our new Prince and Princess of Wales will, I know, continue to inspire and lead our national conversations, helping to bring the marginal to the centre ground where vital help can be given.

'I want also to express my love for Harry and Meghan as they continue to build their lives overseas.'

The day after Charles was crowned, the Coronation Concert took place at Windsor Castle. Prince William made his own pledge of service to his father: 'As my grandmother said when she was crowned, coronations are a declaration of our hopes for the future. And I know she's up there, fondly keeping an eye on us. She would be a very proud mother. For all that celebrations are magnificent, at the heart of the pageantry is a simple message: service. My father's first words on entering Westminster Abbey yesterday were a pledge of service. It was a pledge to continue to serve … Pa, we are all so proud of you.' He ended, 'I commit myself to serve you all – King, country, and Commonwealth. God save the King!'

On the strained relations with his younger son and wife following the Duke and Duchess of Sussex's interview with Oprah Winfrey, Netflix series and the publication of Prince Harry's memoir *Spare*, the King has followed his mother's example. In public at least, he has made no comment.

Grandpa Wales

When it came to becoming a grandparent, Charles drew on his own close relationship with his 'Magical Grandmother'. That relationship was very different from the rigid demands of royal protocol that dictated how he had to behave as a little child. Before he was three, Prince Charles learned to bow before getting a kiss from Gan Gan, his great-grandmother Queen Mary, and not to sit down until asked when in the presence of his grandfather King George.

After the announcement of the birth of Prince George on 22 July 2013, Charles commented on the special moment, 'Grandparenthood is a unique moment in anyone's life, as countless kind people have told me in recent months, so I am enormously proud and happy to be a grandfather for the first time and we are eagerly looking forward to seeing the baby in the near future.'

For his young grandson Charles restored a tree house at Highgrove that Princes William and Harry had played in as boys, and he has been keen to pass on his love of gardening, telling BBC Radio 4's *Gardeners' Question Time* programme: 'The most important thing is I got George planting a tree or two here, so we planted it together and shovelled in the earth ... And then each time they come you say, "Do you see how much the tree has grown?" or whatever, and you hope that they take an interest.'

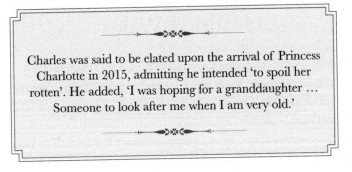

Charles was said to be elated upon the arrival of Princess Charlotte in 2015, admitting he intended 'to spoil her rotten'. He added, 'I was hoping for a granddaughter … Someone to look after me when I am very old.'

When Prince Louis was born in 2018, Charles reflected, 'It is a great joy to have another grandchild. The only trouble is I don't know how I'm going to keep up with them all.'

The King has proved himself an affectionate, hands-on grandfather to his five grandchildren and five step-grandchildren, to whom he is simply 'Grandpa Wales'. The name is a reference to his former title and also echoes Queen Elizabeth II's pet name for her own grandfather, King George V, who she called 'Grandpa England'.

Queen Camilla told how much Charles enjoys reading to them all, especially the Harry Potter books, for which he does all the voices. Speaking on the BBC documentary, *Prince, Son and Heir: Charles at 70*, she admitted, 'He will get down on his knees and crawl about with them for hours, you know making funny noises and laughing, and my grandchildren adore him, absolutely adore him.' He will also help keep them entertained, as demonstrated during the Queen's Platinum Jubilee celebrations when he was happy for a fidgety Prince Louis to clamber onto his lap to watch proceedings.

Speaking on his role as grandfather, Charles explained that he thinks of his own experiences growing up with his beloved grandmother:

'The great thing is to encourage them. Show them things to take their interest. My grandmother did that, she was wonderful. It is very important to create a bond when they are very young.'

The fact that he is unable to spend time with his grandchildren Prince Archie and Princess Lilibet is said to be a source of sorrow for the King.

Having his own grandchildren has made Charles, if anything, an even more passionate advocate for sustainable living and care for our planet in every sense.

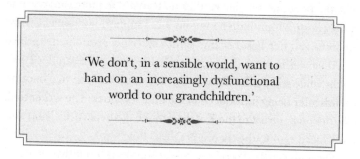

'We don't, in a sensible world, want to hand on an increasingly dysfunctional world to our grandchildren.'

Friends and Mentors

As a young man, Charles was said to have only a few close friends, a trusted inner circle upon whom he relied for their support and discretion. He would spend weekends and holidays away with them reading and relaxing.

When asked about meeting new people, he said, 'You learn through experience how to sense who are the ones that are sucking up and who are being genuine. But, of course, the trouble is that very often the worst people come up first and the really nice people hang back.' He knew that the fact he was royal and Prince of Wales often hampered genuine communication: 'One finds you meet people and you have to get through a certain amount of anxiety, or nervousness, or prejudice or whatever, to start with, and it usually takes about twenty minutes or so before people are beginning to relax ... and then you've got to go.'

Keenly aware of his unique position and inspired by a desire to make a difference, he often looked to older mentors as role models. Key among these were his great-uncle Lord Louis Mountbatten, the author, documentary film-maker and lecturer Laurens van der Post and the poet and scholar Katherine Raine. He increasingly came to rely upon Mountbatten for emotional support and advice, while Laurens van der Post became something of a guru for the prince when he was in his early twenties. Charles first read van der Post's books while still a schoolboy at Gordonstoun and the two became friends after being introduced in the mid-seventies. The writer took Charles on a retreat to the Kalahari to see the 'real Africa' and also introduced him to the theories of Carl Jung.

Through van der Post, Charles met Kathleen Raine, who became another big influence on the young prince. He delivered one of the eulogies at her memorial service in 2003:

'She was always there for me because above all she understood what I was about ... She confessed she had never given the subject of the position I happen to occupy any thought until I came into her life. But her thought then was not "how wonderful to be royal" but "that poor young man, he has the most difficult task in England" ... She [told me that if] during her remaining time here she could play a part in supporting me in realizing my vision of a better world, it would be her greatest happiness. Her advice would come thick and fast: "Dear, dear Prince, don't give that riffraff an inch of ground, not a hair's breadth, stand firm on the holy ground

of the heart. The only way to deal with the evil forces of their world is from a higher level, not to meet them on their own."
This was advice I concurred with wholeheartedly, and still do.'

On Loss

Charles's close emotional bond with his great-uncle Lord Louis Mountbatten is obvious from the many personal letters written between the two over the years. His deep sorrow and shock at his uncle's death on 27 August 1979 is shown in his diary entry for the day which reads, 'I had always dreaded the day when he would die, but somehow I had always thought it would be several more years – at least until he felt "ready" and no longer felt there was anything to go on living for. Life has to go on, I suppose, but this afternoon I must confess I wanted it to stop …'

His affection for Lord Mountbatten was clear:

'I have lost someone infinitely special in my life; someone who showed enormous affection, who told me unpleasant things I didn't particularly want to hear, who gave praise where it was due as well as criticism, someone to whom I knew I could confide anything and from whom I would receive the wisest of counsel and advice. In some extraordinary way he combined grandfather, father, brother, and friend and I shall always be eternally grateful that I was lucky enough to have known him for as long as I did.'

Visiting Mullaghmore Harbour in County Sligo, Ireland where Lord Mountbatten, his grandson, the mother of his son-in-law, and a local teenage boat crew member had died, Charles reflected on the devastation he had felt at the loss: 'I could not imagine how we would come to terms with the anguish of such a deep loss since, for me, Lord Mountbatten represented the grandfather I never had. So, it seemed as if the foundations of all that we held dear in life had been torn apart irreparably ...

'I now understand in a profound way the agonies borne by so many others in these islands, of whatever faith, denomination or political tradition.'

'*You only have to look at Shakespeare's plays, Henry V or Henry IV Parts I and II, to see the change that can take place, because if you become the sovereign, then you play the role in the way it is expected.*'

<small>CHARLES SPEAKING ON THE DIFFERENCE BETWEEN THE ROLES OF PRINCE AND KING IN THE DOCUMENTARY *PRINCE, SON AND HEIR: CHARLES AT 70*.</small>

Crowned

The coronation took place on Saturday 6 May 2023, with Charles and Camilla crowned as King and Queen of the United Kingdom and Commonwealth. Westminster Abbey has been Britain's coronation church since 1066 and King Charles III became the fortieth monarch to be crowned there. The coronation itself is a centuries-old ritual with a Christian service at its heart, during which the new King pledged the statutory coronation oath and was then anointed with oil.

> *'I Charles do solemnly and sincerely in the presence of God profess, testify, and declare that I am a faithful Protestant, and that I will, according to the true intent of the enactments which secure the Protestant succession to the Throne, uphold and maintain the said enactments to the best of my powers according to law,' he said as he knelt before the altar and offered a prayer. 'Grant that I may be a blessing to all thy children, of every faith and belief, that together we may discover the ways of gentleness and be led into the paths of peace.'*

After this, during the investiture King Charles was presented with the various symbolic items of regalia including the Sovereign's Sceptre, Orb and Sword of State. Finally, the Archbishop of Canterbury placed on his head the St Edward's Crown, which was originally commissioned for his namesake King Charles II. This was followed by the customary shouts of 'God Save the King'.

The crowned King then sat on the throne. Historically princes and peers would then kneel to pay homage and swear allegiance; for King Charles this was slightly different. First came the Church of England led by Archbishop Justin Welby, then Prince William performed the 'homage of royal blood'. This was the part played by Prince Philip at Queen Elizabeth II's coronation in 1953.

Prince William declared, 'I, William, Prince of Wales, pledge my loyalty to you and faith and truth I will bear unto you, as your liege man of life and limb. So help me God.'

Lastly came the 'homage of the people' with the congregation invited to take part. Queen Camilla was crowned with Queen Mary's Crown after the ceremony for the King.

After the service there was a state procession to Buckingham Palace with appearances on the balcony, and a concert at Windsor Castle the following day. Across the country street parties and commemorative church services were held, along with other events, including the Big Help Out volunteering day.

Large crowds turned out to watch events and celebrate but there were also protests from republican groups, and the police made several arrests. It is estimated the coronation service drew a peak audience of 20.4 million in the UK.

One year on from his accession to the throne, King Charles spent the anniversary of his mother Queen Elizabeth II's death quietly at Balmoral. There were no public events marking the day, but the King and Queen attended a special service of commemoration at Crathie Kirk. King Charles also recorded a short message in tribute:

'In marking the first anniversary of Her Late Majesty's death and my accession, we recall with great affection her long life, devoted service and all she meant to so many of us.

'I am deeply grateful, too, for the love and support that has been shown to my wife and myself during this year as we do our utmost to be of service to you all.'

Bibliography and Sources

Bedell Smith, Sally, *Charles: The Misunderstood Prince*, Penguin Random House, 2017

Benson, Ross, *Charles: The Untold Story*, Gollancz, 1993

Bower, Tom, *Rebel Prince: The Power, Passion and Defiance of Prince Charles*, William Collins, 2018

Brandreth, Gyles, *Philip and Elizabeth: Portrait of a Marriage*, Arrow Books, 2004

Brown, Tina, *The Palace Papers*, Penguin Random House, 2022

Carlisle, Sam (compiled by), *King Charles III: 100 moments from his journey to the throne*, HarperCollins, 2023

Dimbleby, Jonathan, *The Prince of Wales: A Biography*, Little Brown and Company, 1994

Dolby, Karen, *Queen Elizabeth II's Guide to Life*, Michael O'Mara, 2019

Dolby, Karen, *The Wicked Wit of Prince Philip*, Michael O'Mara, 2017

Dolby, Karen, *The Wicked Wit of the Royal Family*, Michael O'Mara, 2019

Hardman, Robert, *Queen of the World*, Century, 2018

Holden, Anthony, *Prince Charles: A Biography*, Bantam Press, 1998

HRH the Prince of Wales, *A Vision of Britain: A Personal View of Architecture*, Doubleday, 1989

HRH the Prince of Wales and Clover, Charles, *Highgrove: Portrait of an Estate*, Orion Publishing, 1994

James, Alison, *King Charles III: A Modern Monarch*, Sona Books, 2023

Jobson, Robert, *Our King: Charles III: The Man and the Monarch Revealed*, John Blake Publishing, 2023

Junor, Penny, *The Firm: The Troubled Life of the House of Windsor*, HarperCollins, 2011

Levin, Angela, *Camilla: Duchess of Cornwall: From Outcast to Future Queen Consort*, Simon and Schuster, 2022

Marr, Andrew, *The Diamond Queen: Elizabeth II and Her People*, Macmillan UK, 2011

Mayer, Catherine, *Charles: The Heart of a King*, WH Allen, 2015

Morton, Andrew, *Diana: Her True Story – In Her Own Words*, Michael O'Mara, 1992

Petrella, Kate, *Royal Wisdom: The Most Daft, Cheeky and Brilliant Quotes from Britain's Royal Family*, Adams Media, 2011

Sinclair, Marianne and Litvinoff, Sarah (ed), *The Wit and Wisdom of the Royal Family: A Book of Royal Quotes*, Plexus Publishing, 1990

Documentaries

Charles: The Private Man, The Public Role (ITV 1994)

Monarchy: The Royal Family at Work (BBC 2007/2008)

Charles at 60: The Passionate Prince (BBC 2008)

Elizabeth at 90 – A Family Tribute (BBC 2016)

Prince, Son and Heir: Charles at 70 (BBC 2018)

Queen of the World (HBO 2018)

Prince Philip: The Royal Family Remembers (BBC 2021)

Elizabeth: The Unseen Queen (BBC 2022)

Charles R: The Making of a Monarch (BBC 2023)

Charles: In His Own Words (National Geographic 2023)

Websites

bbc.co.uk
brainyquote.com
cbsnews.com
cnn.com
commonslibrary.parliament.uk
dailymail.co.uk
dailyrecord.co.uk
economictimes.com

express.co.uk
famousquotesandauthors.com
forbes.com
gq-magazine.co.uk
harmoniesmagazine.com
harpers.org
harpersbazaar.com
hellomagazine.com

historyextra.com
houseandgarden.co.uk
huffingtonpost.co.uk
imdb.com
independent.co.uk
inews.co.uk
insider.com
itv.com
metro.co.uk
mirror.co.uk
nationalgeographic.com
news.sky.com
newsweek.com
nytimes.com
rct.uk
reuters.com
royal.uk
standard.co.uk

tatler.com
telegraph.co.uk
thedailybeast.com
theguardian.com
thenews.com
thesun.co.uk
thetimes.co.uk
thinkexist.com
time.com
townandcountrymag.com
usatoday.com
usmagazine.com
vanityfair.com
washingtonpost.com
wikipedia.org
yougov.co.uk
youtube.com

Picture Credits

The publisher would like to thank the following for their kind permission to reproduce the following pictures in this book.

p17 Keystone Press/Alamy Stock Photo; p31 Keystone Press/Alamy Stock Photo; p45 PA Images/Alamy Stock Photo; p65 PA Images/Alamy Stock Photo; p89 PA Images/Alamy Stock Photo; p97 Abaca Press/Alamy Stock Photo; p113 Mike Walker/Alamy Stock Photo; p129 PA Images/Alamy Stock Photo; p155 Ian Shaw/Alamy Stock Photo

Every effort has been made to correctly acknowledge the source/or copyright holder and any unintentional errors will be corrected in future editions.